Negotiation, Reciprocity, & Knowledge Sharing

Louis M. Helm

TABLE OF CONTENTS

ABSTRACT____**vi**

Chapter1:Enhancing Knowledge Sharing in Software Teams_______________________________________**1**

Chapter2:Understanding Knowledge Sharing in IT Teams:________________________________**34**

CHAPTER 3. Methodology Overview: Knowledge Sharing Study_______________________________**123**

Abstract

Knowledge sharing among software developers enhances the success of software design and implementation. However, there is an inadequate understanding of how communication factors such as negotiation and reciprocity impact the knowledge-sharing process within software development teams and between team leaders and team members. The present study used a correlational research design to test the relationship between the reciprocity (i.e., communication between team members), negotiation (i.e., communication between team leaders and team members), and knowledge sharing to determine whether different types of communication influence knowledge-sharing outcomes. A cross-sectional survey was used to collect data from a target population of software developers. The sample consisted of 85 software developers with a minimum of 2 years of experience working on software development teams. Multiple linear regression analyses were run to determine the extent to which the variables of negotiation, reciprocity, and knowledge sharing were related. The results indicated that the variables were significantly related, and 70% of knowledge sharing was the result of reciprocity-exchange of ideas and reciprocity-meetings. Team meetings and the open exchange of ideas between team members were found to be the most effective methods of reciprocity related to knowledge sharing among team members. Negotiation and team cohesiveness, however, were not significant to the knowledge-sharing process. The findings indicated that the process of knowledge sharing is more important than individual relationships between software development team members. Thus, from an organizational perspective, holding regular project meetings with all team members would be a more effective knowledge-sharing strategy than using team-building exercises to strengthen personal bonds between team members. Additional research is necessary to determine how software developers' personal characteristics impact knowledge-sharing processes.

CHAPTER 1. Enhancing Knowledge Sharing in Software Teams:

This study was undertaken to investigate how different types of communication affect the knowledge-sharing process in software development teams. Drawing on previous research and theory regarding knowledge sharing from a number of sources (see Joseph, Ocasio, &

McDonnell, 2014; Juiz & Toomey, 2015; Peters & Romi, 2014; Sugumaran, Al-Mutawah, & AlKhaja, 2015; Shelly, Straub, & Liang, 2015), this study explored the vertical knowledge-sharing process of negotiation and the horizontal knowledge-sharing process of reciprocity. Negotiation specifically referred to vertical interactions between IT governance and IT software developers. In the present study, IT governance referred to individuals within an organization responsible for making decisions and overseeing software development teams (e.g., team leaders, IT managers, and senior IT management). This study also explored reciprocity between software development team members in the context of knowledge sharing behaviors. Reciprocity referred to knowledge-sharing processes such as reciprocity-exchange of ideas, reciprocity-meetings, and reciprocity-cohesiveness that occur horizontally between team members.

This chapter serves as an introduction to the study. The first section of the chapter provides important background information related to the problem under study. This section is followed by the statement of the problem. Next, the specific purpose of the study is discussed, followed by an examination of the study' significance to scholarly knowledge and practice. The research questions that were developed to address the problem are then identified along with definitions of relevant terms. A brief outline of the research design follows, with sections on the assumptions and limitations of the research. The chapter concludes with a description of the organization of the remainder of the study.

Background of the Problem

IT software development projects often fail. The overall investment in software development projects in the United States in 2015 was more than 300 billion dollars (Ozer & Vogel, 2015), and the cost of failed IT projects has been estimated to exceed $78 billion annually in the United States (Standish Group, 2014). Experts have argued that the failure of these projects is partly due to inadequate knowledge sharing among IT development staff (Colnar & Dimovski, 2017). Research indicates that critical technical knowledge is often hidden or hoarded by software development team members (Connelly, Zweig, Webster, & Trougakos, 2012), and an unwillingness to share knowledge freely within a development team can lead to the repetition of costly technical errors (Aarnio, 2015; Kang et al., 2013; Zidane & Andersen, 2018).

One way that organizations attempt to reduce software project failure rates is to promote communication and encourage both team leaders and team members to participate in effective knowledge-sharing processes. More effective knowledge sharing can be accomplished through negotiation between IT governance personnel and software development teams as well as through reciprocity between team members. IT governance refers to a technical or administrative entity or person responsible for creating a process of knowledge sharing among all members of software development teams (Williams & Karahanna, 2013). The role of IT governance is to coordinate and create synergy between personnel responsible for system applications, database administration, production support, and security (Altemimi & Mohamad, 2015; Selig, 2016;

Williams & Karahanna, 2013).

The literature on IT governance and software development suggests both the importance of IT governance to project success and a scarcity of empirical data regarding the process of knowledge sharing between IT governance leaders and software development team members (Juiz &

Toomey, 2015; Sandhawalia & Dalcher, 2015). Effective IT governance is essential to ensure the successful development and implementation of an IT application (Schroeder, Pauleen, & Huff, 2012). Altemimi and Mohamad (2015) and Selig (2016) both suggested that IT governance should focus on the performance of IT teams within the context of project resources. Robichau (2011) argued that while IT governance functions as a central organizing unit, there is a need for a concise description of the particular role of individuals working in IT governance. Understanding the negotiation process between IT governance personnel and software development team members could help form that description.

Ghobadi (2015) reviewed literature between 1993 and 2011 and conducted a narrative analysis of IT articles. Ghobadi found only 14% of the participating companies actively promoted knowledge-sharing processes. According to Ghobadi's research, IT governance personnel help develop and manage processes to capture the technical knowledge of different software developers to enhance the knowledge-sharing process. Prior to Ghobadi's research, Martin (2012) asserted that the role of IT governance personnel was to promote knowledge sharing among software developers.

Communication and knowledge sharing between team leaders (i.e., IT governance) and team members is typically referred to as vertical communication or negotiation (Banks et al., 2014). This type of communication is not the only way that knowledge can be shared in software development teams. In the context of IT, the term knowledge sharing is often to describe the exchange of technical information via interactions between IT team members (Olaniran, 2017), and the goal of knowledge sharing is to improve successful project implementation. Knowledge sharing between team members is considered to be horizontal communication, and this type of knowledge sharing is called reciprocity (Banks et al., 2014). Software developers effectively share information through the cooperative exchange of data, files, and techniques to solve technical challenges (Olaniran, 2017). Robichau (2011) noted, however, that the process of knowledge sharing between software developers is often inefficient, and inefficient communication increases IT software development failure rates and associated costs (Connelly et al., 2012).

According to Ghobadi (2015), there was a gap in the literature regarding what scholars know about the knowledge-sharing process. The present study addressed this gap by focusing on problems related to the knowledge-sharing process in IT software development teams (see

Arazy, Gellatly, Brainin, & Nov, 2016; Huang & Zhang, 2016; Mangalaraj, Nerur, Mahapatra, & Price, 2014). Many different theories have been proposed by scholars to explain interaction and knowledge sharing in workplace settings (Choi, 2016; de Jong, Curşeu, & Leenders, 2014; Sollitto, Martin, Dusic, Gibbons, & Wagenhouser, 2016). The present study utilized elements of the leader-member exchange (LMX) theory (Dansereau, Graen, & Haga, 1975; Sollitto et al.,

2016); the team-member exchange (TMX) theory (Banks et al., 2014; Seers, 1989); and

Nonaka's (1994) knowledge sharing theory.

Interaction among individuals at different hierarchical levels is the primary focus of the LMX theory (Dansereau et al., 1975; Sollitto et al., 2016). Conversely, the TMX theory addresses knowledge sharing and interaction between peers (Banks et al., 2014; Seers, 1989). In the LMX theory, the interaction is described as negotiation; in the TMX theory, the interaction is described as reciprocity. Figure 1 presents a visual representation of a combination of the LMX theory and the TMX theory regarding knowledge sharing. Many different scholars have used these studies in an attempt to understand interactions among members of IT governance and software development teams (Habjan & Pucihar, 2017; Hoefer & Green, 2016; Ojala, 2016; Xiaojun, 2017). Chapter 2 presents a detailed discussion of these theories and their relation to the knowledge-sharing process.

Figure 1. Research model.

Statement of the Problem

The generic problem was the gap in the literature regarding the knowledge-sharing process among software developers. While some researchers have focused on describing and defining the role of IT governance (Altemimi & Mohamad, 2015; Benaroch & Chernobai, 2017; Juiz & Toomey, 2015; Olaniran, 2017; Robichau, 2011; Sandhawalia & Dalcher, 2015;

Schroeder et al., 2012; Selig, 2016; Williams & Karahanna, 2013), other investigators sought to describe the role of knowledge sharing in IT environments (Connelly et al., 2012;

Nandedkar & Deshpande, 2012; Phelps, Heidl, & Wadhwa, 2012; Sandhawalia & Dalcher, 2015). Another group of researchers focused on defining tacit and explicit knowledge sharing (Boden, Avram, Bannon, & Wulf, 2012; Chen, Hsu, Wang, & Lin, 2011; Deng & Davidson, 2013; Ghobadi,

2015; Martin, 2012; Olaniran, 2017; Mustapha, 2012; Ozer & Vogel, 2015; Parviainen & Tihinen, 2014; Pernstal, Magazinius, & Gorschek, 2012; Rui-Yang & Chao-Tsong, 2015;

Sandhawalia & Dalcher, 2015; Schoenherr, Griffith, & Chandra, 2014; Schroeder et al., 2012).

Researchers also focused on the differences between vertical and horizontal knowledge exchange (Altemimi & Mohamad, 2015; Banks et al., 2014; Benaroch & Chernobai, 2017; Schoenherr et al., 2014; Selig, 2016; Shelly et al., 2015; Stanciu & Tinca, 2017).

Despite the many studies focused on knowledge-sharing processes in an IT context, there remains a lack of clarity as to how negotiation and reciprocity influence the knowledge-sharing process within software development teams (Banks et al., 2014; Benaroch & Chernobai, 2017). To address the knowledge gaps, this researcher evaluated two specific knowledge-sharing processes within software development teams: (a) the vertical knowledge-sharing process between IT governance personnel and software developers (i.e., negotiation) and (b) the horizontal knowledge-sharing process among software developers (i.e., reciprocity). By evaluating these factors, the present study addressed a gap in the body of knowledge and extended the research by Sollitto et al. (2016) and de Jong et al. (2014).

Purpose of the Study

The purpose of this quantitative, nonexperimental, multiple regression analyses was to measure the impact of negotiation and reciprocity on the knowledge-sharing within software development teams. Many researchers have noted the necessity of exploring the relationship between negotiation with IT governance and knowledge sharing among software developers

(Altemimi & Mohamad, 2015; Benaroch & Chernobai, 2017; Juiz & Toomey, 2015; Olaniran,

2017; Robichau, 2011; Sandhawalia & Dalcher, 2015; Schroeder et al., 2012; Selig, 2016; Williams & Karahanna, 2013). Researchers have also recognized the importance of studying horizontal knowledge-sharing through different types of reciprocity among software developers, (Buvik & Tvedt, 2017; Chun, Cho, & Sosik, 2016; Deng, Leung, Lam, & Huang, 2017; Huang, Chang, & Wu, 2017; Yoshikawa, 2017). Despite the level of scholarly interest in this topic, the process of effective knowledge sharing remains unclear. Thus, the purpose of this study was to address the gap in the literature about (a) the vertical interaction process between IT governance members and software developers (i.e., negotiation) and (b) the horizontal interaction process of knowledge sharing among software developers (i.e., reciprocity).

Significance of the Study

This research was significant because it added to the scholarly understanding of knowledge sharing within software development teams. Ghobadi (2015); Hau, Kim, Lee, and Kim (2013); Lindner and Wald (2011); and Phelps et al. (2012) investigated knowledge sharing among software developers and acknowledged the need to discover more effective ways for software developers to share and contribute knowledge when they are working on projects. Furthermore, other scholars have noted that IT governance influences both the selection of team members and the knowledge-sharing process among software developers (Altemimi &

Mohamad, 2015; Benaroch & Chernobai, 2017; Ozer & Vogel, 2015; Selig, 2016; Shelly et al., 2015). The present research offers insights into the horizontal process of knowledge sharing among team members. The present study also addresses the role of IT governance members and explores how vertical knowledge-sharing processes affect the software developers. Organizations could use the results to improve software project outcomes by reducing project failure rates (Banks et al., 2014).

The present study was also significant because it offered information about the elements of tacit and explicit knowledge-sharing process among software developers. According to

Sandhawalia and Dalcher (2015), sharing both tacit and explicit knowledge is an important part of maintaining social relationships in project groups. The present study provided insights into how software developers process knowledge through social activities. The information obtained could help improve software developers' social interactions with IT governance members, which, in turn, could facilitate the production of more reliable software applications and reduce the number of failed projects (Aleksić, Stanisavljević, & Bošković, 2016; Cantor, Morrow, & Blackhurst, 2015; Dalton, Davis, & Viator, 2015).

The study was also significant in that it may lead to more effective project management and knowledge-sharing tools in the field of software development. Several software packages to facilitate software development projects already exist for software development. One example of a software package that facilitates interaction among users and software development programs is Agile (Baham, Hirschheim, Calderon, & Kisekka, 2017; Hoffer, George, & Valacich, 2014; Wen-Lung, Chung-Yang, & Chun-Shuo, 2018). While Agile can help software development teams design and build IT applications within budget and on schedule, the primary goal of the present study was to better understand the process of knowledge sharing, not the use of project management tools. A better understanding of how negotiation and reciprocity influences knowledge sharing among software developers would allow IT governance personnel to mitigate knowledge-sharing challenges that might undermine project success (Barnett, Jones, Bennett, Iverson, & Bonney, 2012;

Juiz & Toomey, 2015). This understanding would also allow IT governance personnel to develop more effective tools that account for different knowledgesharing processes as part of project management, reducing the number of failed software development projects.

Research Questions

Primary Research Question

Research Question. To what extent do negotiation and reciprocity relate to knowledge sharing among software developers?

Research Subquestions

Research Subquestion 1. To what extent is the software developers' negotiation with IT governance related to knowledge sharing among team members?

Research Subquestion 2. To what extent are the reciprocity-exchange of ideas with other software developers related to knowledge sharing among team members'?

Research Subquestion 3. To what extent are the reciprocity-meetings with other software developers related to knowledge sharing among team members?

Research Subquestion 4. To what extent is reciprocity-cohesiveness of a software development team related to knowledge sharing among software development team members?

Definition of Terms

Exchange of ideas in software development. An exchange of ideas is the process where software developers discuss, trade, explore, and freely interchange ideas and information to reach consensus about a software development project (Bergeron, Shipp, Rosen, & Furst, 2013; Lee, 2015; Tang, Shang, Naumann, & Zedtwitz, 2014).

Explicit knowledge. Explicit knowledge is the conscious understanding of information that people easily transfer or distribute in oral or written form (Schoenherr et al.,

2014). People distribute explicit knowledge in books, instructions, or codes (Hau et al., 2013; Nonaka, 1994; Polanyi, 1967).

Information technology (IT) governance. IT governance refers to the people who oversee the technical and administrative entities in organizations (Nicho & Khan, 2017).

Information technology (IT) governance goal. The main goal of those working in IT governance is to create a process of knowledge sharing among software team members (Selig, 2016; Shelly et al., 2015).

Knowledge sharing. In IT, knowledge sharing is the exchange of information intended to enhance the interactions between IT team members (Olaniran, 2017). The operational definition of knowledge sharing referred to the process of acquiring and sharing knowledge that can impact the design and development of software applications used for data storage and retrieval and for making business decisions.

Knowledge. In IT, knowledge is the consolidation of data and information, both tacit and explicit, regarding what, how, why, and who is involved to solve a problem (Hau et al., 2013; Nonaka, 1994; Phelps et al., 2012; Polanyi, 1967; Stanciu & Tinca, 2017; Z. Y. Wu, Ming, He,

Li, & Li, 2014).

Negotiation. Negotiation is a dialogue between an IT governance member and a

software developer with the intent to resolve a conflict or reach a compromise (Schoenherr et al., 2014; Stanciu & Tinca, 2017). The operational definition of negotiation referred to the process between a member of IT governance and a programmer that can impact knowledge sharing between software developers to produce corporate applications that employees use for data storage and retrieval and for making business decisions.

Participant characteristics. Qualtrics randomly selected participants from its participant database using inclusion criteria the researcher provided to the survey company. Qualtrics emailed database members who met the selection criteria providing them with a link to a Web page that explained the purpose of the study and invited them to participate. Each participant needed to (a) be United States citizens, (b) be working on a software development team as a programmer, (c) have a minimum of a two-year college degree, and (d) have a minimum of two years of experience in their role as a programmer.

Reciprocity. Reciprocity among software developers is a mutually beneficial exchange of ideas (Buvik & Tvedt, 2017; Chun et al., 2016; Deng et al., 2017; Yoshikawa, 2017).

Reciprocity-cohesiveness. Reciprocity-cohesiveness refers to a sense of unity within a software development team. The cohesiveness of software team members is based on the social and mental models that facilitate technical discussion and assist in solving design challenges (Havakhor & Sabherwal, 2018). The operational definition of reciprocity-cohesiveness referred to the common characteristics of a group of software developers based on the social interaction, perceived unity, social history, and emotions intimacy. Reciprocity-cohesiveness between software developers for sharing tacit and explicit knowledge can impact the creation of software applications that are used for data storage and retrieval and for making business decisions.

Reciprocity-exchange of ideas. Reciprocity-exchange of ideas refers to the transfer of knowledge from one team member to another. Social norms obligate software developers to return technical help they receive to the provider. The action of the knowledge provider is instigated by the anticipation that reciprocated technical assistance will be available when it is needed (Huang, Tafti, & Mithas, 2018). The operational definition of reciprocity-exchange of ideas referred to the process of technical conversation between software developers for sharing tacit and explicit knowledge that impact the creation of software applications used by corporate employees for data storage and retrieval and for making business decisions.

Reciprocity-meetings. Reciprocity-meetings refers to knowledge sharing that occurs during gatherings attended by software development team members. During these meetings, software developers deliberate on project issues and solve technical problems (Seers, 1989). The operational definition of reciprocity-meetings referred to the process of assembling software developers to engage in sharing tacit and explicit knowledge that can impact the creation of software applications for data storage and retrieval and for making business decisions.

Sample. According to US-Software-Developers (2012), there were around 1,020,000 software developers in 2012 in the United States. From the population of 1,020,000 software developers, Qualtrics indicated that their member database contained a total of 17,640 verified software developers that met the study's selection criteria. From the sample frame of 17,640 verified software developers, Qualtrics recruited 85 programmers who met the selection criteria

Tacit knowledge. Tacit knowledge is the implicit intellectual understanding used to solve a software problem (Choi, 2016; Nonaka, 1994; Polanyi, 1967).

Variables. By using the research chosen research design, the researcher could quantify the impact of the independent variables of negotiation and reciprocity on the dependent variable of knowledge sharing (see Field, 2013; Sekaran & Bougie, 2014; Vogt, 2007). Additionally, reciprocity has three sub variables: reciprocity-exchange of ideas, reciprocity-meetings, and reciprocity-cohesiveness.

Research Design

This inquiry used a nonexperimental, quantitative research design to examine the knowledge-sharing process among IT governance personnel and software developers. The researcher adopted and merged the LMX theory, the TMX theory, and the knowledge-sharing theory to create a theoretical lens. A cross-sectional survey instrument that included elements of the TMX, the LMX-7, and Nonaka's Knowledge Sharing Questionnaire was used to measure participants' experiences related to knowledge sharing. Survey data was collected and analyzed using SPSS, and a multiple linear analysis was used to determine the significance of the relationships between negotiation and reciprocity and knowledge sharing. The use of previously validated instruments and the random selection of participants were incorporated into the study's research design to ensure that viable data was produced (Field, 2013; Moqbel, Nevo, & Kock, 2013; Vogt, 2007).

Qualtrics, an online survey company, randomly recruited 85 U.S. software developers to respond to questions related to their relationships with management (i.e., IT governance) and their peers (i.e., team members). Negotiation, the interaction between IT governance members and software developers, and reciprocity, the interaction between software development team members, functioned as the study's independent variables. Knowledge sharing served as the dependent variable. The information obtained from this investigation was expected to help improve IT governance, facilitate the production of more reliable software applications, and reduce the number of failed projects (Aleksić et al., 2016; Cantor et al., 2015; Dalton et al., 2015).

Assumptions and Limitations

Assumptions

The researcher made several assumptions when selecting a quantitative nonexperimental research design. Some of the assumptions related to the methods used to conduct the study. The researcher used a survey to collect responses from participants about knowledge-sharing behaviors of software developers and IT governance members. This methodological approach relied on the assumption that the participants would select a reasonable matching response from the survey items to represent their experiences. Sollitto et al. (2016), de Jong et al. (2014), and Choi (2016) used similar surveys and data collection methods. Furthermore, the researcher assumed that the participants would respond to the online survey questionnaire honestly and that it was possible to generalize participants' responses to larger, comparable populations (Field, 2013; George, Chiba, & Scheepers, 2017; Sekaran & Bougie, 2014; Vogt, 2007).

In addition to the methodological assumptions, the study also included theoretical assumptions. The researcher relied on existing theories to create the study's theoretical framework: (a) the LMX theory (Dansereau et al., 1975); (b) the TMX theory (Seers, 1989), and (c) knowledge-sharing theory (Nonaka, 1994). This reliance meant that the assumptions inherent in those theories also applied to the present study. The primary assumption of the LMX theory is that an employee is a member of either an in-group or an out-group (Dansereau et al., 1975). The primary assumption of the TMX theory is that reciprocity-exchange of ideas, reciprocitymeetings, and reciprocity-cohesiveness impact software developers (Farmer, Van Dyne, & Kamdar, 2015; Seers, 1989). The primary assumption of the knowledge-sharing theory is that individuals from different cultural backgrounds can use similar knowledge-sharing processes (Huo, Zhang, & Guo, 2016; Su, 2015). The researcher also assumed that negotiation and reciprocity stimulate the knowledge-sharing process among software developers.

The researcher also made topic-specific assumptions. The researcher assumed that a low level of knowledge sharing would impede the successful development of software applications. Conversely, the researcher assumed that improved knowledge-sharing processes (a) among software developers and (b) between software developers and IT governance would result in more successful software development outcomes. These assumptions supported the need to investigate knowledge sharing further in this context. The researcher based these assumptions on earlier work by Joseph et al. (2014), Juiz and Toomey (2015), Peters and Romi (2014), and

Sugumaran et al. (2015).

The survey instrument used to collect the data combined elements from three previously validated instruments. Recent research supports the use of these instruments. Sollitto et al. (2016) used the LMX instrument, de Jong et al. (2014) used the TMX instrument, and Choi (2016) used Nonaka's knowledge-sharing instrument. Therefore, the researcher assumed that the consolidated instrument was valid and reliable. To test this assumption and validate the data collection procedure, the researcher performed a pilot test.

Limitations

Two primary limitations resulted from the selection of the research design. First, the researcher did not measure participants' experience or tenure as software developers.

While research does indicate that experience and tenure can influence knowledge sharing (Kucharska & Kowalczyk, 2016), limitations related to the sample frame did not allow for a stratified sample of software developers with various levels of experience. Instead, participants were required to have a minimum of 2 years of experience working as a software developer. Additionally, IT governance members were also not screened based on their qualifications or tenure.

The second design limitation was related to the selection of the theories used to examine the knowledge-sharing process. Stewart, May, and Ledgerwood (2015) noted that many leadership theories currently in use are dated and have limitations when applied to younger workers. As a result, the use of the LMX, the TMX, and Nonaka's knowledge-sharing theory meant that the researcher viewed the knowledge-sharing process through a lens that may have emphasized nuances in knowledge-sharing processes among older individuals and minimized the focus on knowledge-sharing behaviors common among younger software developers.

The researcher also identified a small number of delimitations when designing the study. First, this study only included software developers working in the United States. The researcher purposely excluded software developers working in other countries from the study to avoid any chance that cultural influences would affect the knowledge-sharing process. The potential influence of culture was a concern because earlier research showed that cultural differences could affect the knowledge-sharing process (Huo et al., 2016; Stewart et al., 2015; Su, 2015).

A second delimitation was the decision not to include the construct of *knowledge integration* in the research model. Knowledge integration deals with the synthesis of multiple knowledge models (Nonaka, Toyama, & Konno, 2000; Phelps et al., 2012). While knowledge integration can be an essential part of knowledge sharing, it was not fundamental to the knowledge-sharing process as conceptualized in the present study (Tiwari, 2015; T. Wu, Lee, Hu, & Yang, 2014). The researcher focused on the knowledge-sharing process and excluded the concept of knowledge integration from the study to avoid confusion.

The third delimitation was that the study did not address the personality traits of software developers. While other researchers examined the role of personality in knowledge sharing
(Bala, Massey, & Montoya, 2017; Chai, Das, & Rao, 2011; Hirschfeld & Thomas, 2011;
Xiaojun, 2017), the researcher chose to exclude personality as a variable in the present study. The present study's focus was on knowledge sharing from a process-oriented perspective as opposed to an individualistic perspective. Yen (2016) noted that this distinction is important when studying the knowledge-sharing process.

The fourth and final delimitation was that the present study did not address software development tools such as Agile. The focus was on the social aspects of the knowledge-sharing process as opposed to knowledge-sharing techniques facilitated through user interfaces (Ghobadi, 2015; Ozer & Vogel, 2015). The decision to exclude programs like Agile allowed the researcher to focus on interpersonal knowledge sharing among development team members and with IT governance personnel. The research neither included the role of a user nor tested the accuracy of the produced software. Additionally, different organizations could use other methodologies for IT applications' development. For these reasons, the researcher did not include the use of software development programs like Agile in the study's design.

Organization of the Remainder of the Study

Chapter 1 addressed the background of the problem, the statement of the problem, the purpose of the study, the significance of the study, the research questions, definitions of terms, the research design, and assumptions and limitations. Chapter 2 presents a review of the literature on the topic of knowledge sharing within IT and software development teams. Chapter 3 addresses the study's theoretical framework, methods, and ethical considerations. Chapter 4 contains a description of the results of the data analysis. Chapter 5 includes a discussion of the research findings in connection with relevant literature and suggestions for future research.

CHAPTER 2. Understanding Knowledge Sharing in IT Teams

Chapter 2 contains a review of the literature about the topic of knowledge sharing in IT software development teams. The literature review indicated a gap existed regarding what scholars know about negotiation and reciprocity between IT governance personnel and software developers. What follows first is a section about the methods used to search for academic articles on these topics. Other sections of this chapter include the theoretical orientation for the study, the review of the literature, the synthesis of the research findings, and the critique of the research methods. The chapter concludes with a summary section.

Methods of Searching

The goal of this research was to understand better how negotiation with IT governance and reciprocity between IT software developers impacted knowledge-sharing processes.

Databases used to search the literature including Academic Search Premier, Business Expert

Press, Business Market Research Collection, Business Source Complete, Health and Psychosocial Instruments, Mental Measurement Yearbook, and PsycTests. Furthermore, the website Google Scholar offered the researcher access to additional peer-reviewed articles.

Because the term knowledge sharing is broad, the researcher used it along with other, more researchable terms, like *corporate governance, internal controls, corporate structure, knowledge dissemination, IT governance, software developers, negotiation, reciprocity, and team building.* Additionally, combinations of search terms included *information technology, software developers*, and *IT governance, reciprocity*, or *knowledge sharing* to narrow the results of the search. The researcher refined the search parameters to only included articles published within seven years of the date of this study. Furthermore, the researcher retrieved information about the three survey instruments from PsycTESTS and Sage publications. What follows next is a description of the study's theoretical orientation.

Theoretical Orientation for the Study

IT specialists produce knowledge, and that knowledge flourishes through social interactions among software developers (Panda & Kapoor, 2017; Trantopoulos, von Krogh, Wallin, & Woerter, 2017). According to Nonaka (1994) and Choi (2016), knowledge can be both tacit and explicit. In seminal research on knowledge sharing, Polanyi (1967) stated that organizations should encourage and gather both explicit and tacit dimensions of knowledge. Polanyi defined tacit knowledge as knowledge that is known but cannot be told. Tacit knowledge is part of the knowledge a software developer uses to solve problems. Natural tacit knowledge is part of how people learn; tacit knowledge is also part of the fabric of families, communities, and organizations (Potter & Lupilya,

2016). Individuals internalize observations, and in doing so, those observations become tacit knowledge (Carlsen, 2016).

To understand the knowledge-sharing process, the present researcher drew on elements of three different theories. The three theories that provided the theoretical foundation for the present study included the LMX theory (Dansereau et al., 1975); the TMX theory (Seers, 1989); and the knowledge-sharing theory (Nonaka, 1994). The following subsections provide descriptions of each of the theories.

Leader-Member Exchange (LMX) Theory

Building upon Jacobs' (1970) role theory, Dansereau et al. (1975) formulated the LMX theory to describe the nature of the interaction between supervisors and subordinates. Dansereau et al. postulated that due to time limitations, supervisors classify employees into two groups.

Favorite employees belong to what Dansereau et al. termed the in-group, and the other employees belong to the out-group. The LMX theory suggested that supervisors would deal with all employees through formal channels and only connect with favored employees (i.e., the ingroup) through informal channels.

Theorists use the LMX theory to explain, describe, and predict the dynamic relationships between supervisors and employees. The dyadic relationship between a supervisor and an employee determines whether an employee is assigned to an in-group or an out-group. Dansereau et al. (1975) developed four constructs associated with the LMX theory: (a) negotiating latitude, (b) superior's contribution, (c) member's contribution, and (d) outcome. One of the significant advantages of using the constructs of the LMX theory is the ability to predict communication between supervisors and subordinates (Collins & Mossholder, 2017; Connelly & Zweig, 2015; Dienesch & Liden, 1986). In the context of IT software development projects, this communication is considered negotiation between IT governance personnel and development team members.

LMX theory assumptions. While the LMX theory is popular among researchers, one of the theory's weaknesses is the methodological problem that lies in the different operationalizations of LMX across empirical studies (Collins & Mossholder, 2017; Dienesch & Liden, 1986). One of the difficulties of comparing the results of research that used the LMX constructs is that some studies measured two items while others used 12 items (Dienesch &

Liden, 1986). The present study used only a single construct from the LMX theory, negotiation. Many researchers use the LMX concepts of the in-group and the out-group to describe, explain, and predict the dynamic relationships between supervisors and employees.

When developing the LMX theory, Dansereau et al. conducted a quantitative nonexperimental study that surveyed 60 managers working for the housing division of a public university. The authors developed an instrument, which came to be known as the 7-item LMX instrument or the LMX-7. The authors used their questionnaire to collect data via four sets of interviews of all 60 managers. Dansereau et al. also collected data from employees of 17 managers via interviews. The authors classified the employees as members of the in-group or the out-group. The authors claimed that a supervisor would deal with all employees through the formal channels and only have contact with the favorite employees (i.e., those in the in-group) through informal channels.

LMX empirical laws. Kroll (2015) conducted a systematic literature review to identify the major factors of performance elements. According to Kroll, most researchers treated factors of performance information individually rather than collectively (Hahn & Albert, 2017; Lee, 2015; Tang et al., 2014). Kroll indicated that the reviewed articles measured performance individually instead of from the perspective of team performance. One of the major advantages of the LMX is the capability to predict an individual's behavior (Dienesch & Liden, 1986). Graen, Novak, and Sommerkamp (1982) compared the predictive power of the LMX theory with the predictive power of average leadership style (ALS) to determine which theory was more effective at predicting turnover. Graen et al. examined turnover among 48 systems analysts and computer programmers in a large, public utility and found that the LMX theory predicted turnover better than ALS.

LMX theory constructs. LMX constructs allow a member to negotiate (Dansereau et al., 1975), and negotiation is a process that software-developers follow to determine the time and the cost of building a program. Dansereau et al. (1975) indicated that the LMX theory encompassed four constructs: (a) negotiating latitude, (b) superior's contribution, (c) member's contribution, and (d) outcome. This researcher only evaluated the negotiation construct of the LMX theory and applied that construct the interaction between IT governance personnel and software development team members.

According to Benaroch and Chernobai (2017), Lynn and Kalay (2015), Maiello (2014), and Susser (2012), the role of IT governance is to make the company's future vision clear to software developers. Otherwise, the implementation of the constructs of the LMX theory would dissolve into disintegrated efforts with the probability of more software failures. When collecting data, Dansereau et al. (1975) divided employees into two groups based on relationships with their supervisor. There were 29 participants for the in-group, and 31 for the out-group, indicating there was an equal ratio of participants in each group. What follows is a description of TMX theory.

Team-Member Exchange Theory (TMX)

Seers (1989) included reciprocity as a construct for the TMX theory as a measuring unit of cooperation among team members. Seers divided the reciprocity construct into three variables:

(a) reciprocity-exchange of ideas, (b) reciprocity-meetings, and (c) reciprocity-cohesiveness. Seers proposed a construct named team-member exchange quality for the employment role. The scope of each focal role affects the dynamic interpersonal relationship between employees on the same team (Seers, 1989). Seers (1989) based the TMX theory on Jacobs' (1970) role theory and the LMX theory (Dansereau et al., 1975). While researchers use the constructs of the TMX to investigate the nature of the relationship between team members (Seers, 1989), the constructs of the LMX investigate the relationships between supervisors and employees.

Seers, Petty, and Cashman (1995) reported that using the constructs of the TMX improved the performance of an autonomous team in comparison to that of a traditional workgroup. Seers et al. claimed that traditionally there are diverse types of team formations (e.g., manager-lead, self-managing, and self-designing). Seers et al. addressed the concept of peer-role making in contrast to other team formations. With peer-role-making, the relationships between team members are supportively reciprocal, and any member of the role set can receive technical assistance and provide sustainable technical support to other team members. Meeting the expectations of the role sender strengthens and reinforces the relationships between team members. Thus, the team member relationship is egalitarian (Seers et al., 1995), which means a team is characterized by fairness in both responsibility and reward for all the members, and the structure of a team is less hierarchal than the traditional workgroup structure (Seers et al., 1995).

Seers et al. (1995) noted that the participants were divided into teams that were responsible for designing and building components based on the proficiency of the team members. Some IT professionals view software development as a type of artwork (Knuth, 1969). Thus, a self-designing workgroup structure might be most useful for software development. With a self-designing team, the software developers collectively have the full responsibility of securing application requirements, designing, and implementing an application.

TMX assumptions. Seers (1989) developed the TMX theory to explain, describe, and predict the dynamic activities within a group that contribute to team building. The concept was based on peer-role making, and the constructs were quality, job satisfaction, and performance (Seers, 1989). The author conducted the investigation using a two-group quasi-experimental design (Seers et al., 1995). One of the groups consisted of a peer-role making team, and the other group consisted of a traditional team. For the TMX theory to be effective, the quality of the TMX construct would depend on the exchange relationship between a member with a focal role and the rest of the team members (Seers, 1989). If a team has five members, then each focal rolemember will have $N(N-1)/2$ relationships, or $5(5 - 1)/2 = 10$ relationships (Project Management

Institute, 2014).

TMX relationships between team members allow individuals to leverage knowledge (Banks et al., 2014). Combining the vertical relationships described as part of the LMX theory, and the horizontal relationships described as part of the TMX theory could be beneficial for the development of software (Banks et al., 2014). With the constructs of the LMX theory, a supervisor could allocate or deny resources to employees (Banks et al., 2014), but with the constructs of the TMX theory, group members are on equal footing concerning software development resources (Banks et al., 2014). Banks et al. (2014) indicated that the constructs of both the LMX theory and the TMX theory impact the work outcomes process.

TMX empirical laws. According to Kroll (2015), most of the studies using the TMX theory measured performance individually rather than collectively. In contrast, Seers et al. (1995) measured the performance of an entire team. The actions of other members can define a focal role through the reinforcement of reciprocal actions (Jacobs, 1970). Seers (1989) developed the TMX theory using the quality construct to measure the extent of the reciprocity of the interactions between a team member and the rest of the team (Seers, 1989). An IT expert could attest that the constructs of the TMX are critical to a software development team because the constructs of the LMX are less applicable to lower organizational levels (Liden & Graen, 1980; T. Wu et al., 2014). In contrast, the TMX curtails a supervision role and allows a team to carry out its activities autonomously (Seers, 1989).

According to Seers et al. (1995), team members who followed the peer-role making concept could resolve tension and conflict by themselves. Furthermore, the higher the quality of most team exchanges, the more effective the team performance (Seers et al., 1995). Seers et al. said that team-member exchange could overcome some barriers with the selection of a leader for the team (Chiniara & Bentein, 2016). IT governance members can determine the quality of interaction between a focal role member and the other team members with whom the focal role member interacts (Seers, 1989). Therefore, IT governance members could use the TMX quality construct as a predictor of team performance (Seers, 1989). Seers (1989) based the TMX quality construct on mutual support reciprocity within the group, but it is not dependent on the cohesiveness of the entire group. Therefore, the TMX construct could produce data with statistically significant differences (Seers, 1989).

TMX constructs. Researchers can use the TMX quality construct to measure reciprocity between team members (Seers et al., 1995). For example, software developers could use reciprocity-exchange of ideas to identify a software anomaly and solve the problem causing the anomaly. The assessment of each team member's contribution needs to acknowledge the technical assets each member brings to the team as those assets can affect the exchange process (Seers et al., 1995). Thus, knowledge-sharing contributions, not jobholder positions, are the critical factors for success in the development of software applications (Seers et al., 1995). Therefore, the interchange between each member and the rest of the team would reinforce the identity and dynamic of a team (Seers et al., 1995). Members of the team perceive the contributions of other members as integral to group success (Seers et al., 1995).

Knowledge-Sharing Theory

Nonaka (1994) said that the creation of knowledge depends on collaboration among members of a team who share specific knowledge and enjoy independence. Nonaka (1994) introduced four modes (constructs) of knowledge creation: socialization, externalization, internalization, and combination. The present study investigated the interplay process of knowledge sharing among software developers. Pemsel and Wiewiora (2013) claimed that the process of knowledge sharing between software project teams is inefficient. Furthermore, there is no dedicated entity responsible for capturing critical technical knowledge and disseminating it to other project teams to avoid investing resources in technical solutions that already exist (Pemsel & Wiewiora, 2013). The absence of such an entity inhibits knowledge sharing between software developers (Benaroch & Chernobai, 2017).

Sometimes, a critical technical knowledge that is available within a project team is hidden or hoarded from another software development team that needs it (Connelly et al., 2012). To explore how IT governance affects knowledge sharing, Shelly et al. (2015) researched 131 companies and 72 firms. Shelly et al. concluded that the role of IT governance and its relationship with knowledge sharing is neglected in the scholarly literature. Additionally, Benaroch and Chernobai (2017) claimed that the IT experience-level of IT governance members can impact knowledge sharing among software developers, and more experienced IT governance personnel are more effective at avoiding project failures.

According to Sandhawalia and Dalcher (2015), there is a scarcity of literature regarding the sharing of both tacit and explicit knowledge among team members. Ghobadi's (2015) narrative analysis indicated that only 14% of organizations promote knowledge sharing. IT governance can promote technical knowledge sharing, but Fehrenbacher (2017) suggested that IT governance (i.e., management) should be aware of the costs associated with knowledge sharing. Ghobadi (2015) asserted that knowledge is a significant institutional asset that organizations must manage. Ghobadi claimed that IT governance personnel should support the process of creating and sharing knowledge within corporate units including IT software development teams. Ghobadi also advocated for a process that enhances knowledge sharing among software developers. Knowledge starts as intuition or a guess, and it is perceived in the mind of a software developer for solving a technical challenge. Software solutions result from cognitive processing that was prompted by anomalies in the software execution (Nonaka, 1994).

Ozer and Vogel (2015) reported that software knowledge sharing was high in teams with high autonomy and low in teams with low autonomy. According to Sandhawalia and Dalcher (2015), a process of sharing tacit and explicit knowledge facilitates the successful design and implementation of software applications. IT governance enhances tacit knowledge sharing by codifying and storing explicit knowledge in the form of standards (Sandhawalia & Dalcher, 2015). Additionally, the authors argued that tacit knowledge is the foundation of explicit knowledge. Thus, IT governance members should pay particular attention to team social activity processes as those are frequently result in tacit knowledge sharing.

Organizations must promote the process of knowledge sharing regardless of whether the knowledge is tacit or explicit

(Amoako-Gyampah, Meredith, & White Loyd, 2018; Arsenyan & Büyüközkan, 2016; Sandhawalia & Dalcher, 2015). This process is referred to as knowledge integration. Knowledge integration requires assistance and mentoring (Sandhawalia & Dalcher, 2015). IT governance should recognize that a project's success depends on an array of expertise that must be available to software developers (Sandhawalia & Dalcher, 2015). A knowledgeintegration process may require the augmentation of resources of both internal and external skills. Regardless of the processes, the knowledge must be transferred to the project team

(Jandhyala & Phene, 2015; Lim, Jarvenpaa, & Lanham, 2015; Sandhawalia & Dalcher, 2015).

The augmentation of new knowledge processes can help a team deliver a successful project and reduce the likelihood of project failure (Sandhawalia & Dalcher, 2015). IT governance members must be cognizant of the need for specialized technical tasks that require assistance from experts.

IT governance members should establish a process of communication between the expert and a software developer (Sandhawalia & Dalcher, 2015). A process of effective knowledge sharing that flows between software development team members would impact knowledge integration and promote the success of an IT project (Grant, 1996; Schoenherr et al., 2014).

Review of the Literature

This investigator developed the research variables from the research question. The research question guided the literature review. The literature review addressed the independent and dependent variables of negotiation and reciprocity that could influence knowledge sharing among software developers. The first section summarizes the articles pertinent to this study and the use of the constructs of the LMX and TMX theories. The second section is devoted to the selected articles that addressed the independent variable of negotiation between IT governance and software development team members. Next is a section on the independent variable that is reciprocity. Following the description of the independent variables, the researcher reviews research on the dependent variable: knowledge sharing among software developers.

The LMX and the TMX

While the LMX theory and the TMX theory each address relationships between employees, the constructs of each theory are different. The LMX theory describes the vertical relationships between supervisors and subordinates (Dansereau et al., 1975) whereas the TMX defines the horizontal relationships between team members (Seers, 1989). While some researchers have focused on the vertical interaction between supervisors and subordinates, other researchers have investigated the horizontal interactions between members of a team (Altemimi & Mohamad, 2015; Banks et al., 2014; Benaroch & Chernobai, 2017; Cândido & Santos, 2015;

Joseph et al., 2014; Juiz & Toomey, 2015; Peters & Romi, 2014; Schoenherr et al., 2014; Selig, 2016; Shelly et al., 2015; Stanciu & Tinca, 2017; Sugumaran et al., 2015). The following review of the LMX theory and the TMX theory include summaries of selected articles.

Banks et al. (2014) conducted a meta-analysis review and reported the results of several studies. The authors studied the impact of the constructs of the LMX theory and the TMX theory on work outcomes. Banks et al. concluded that their literature review yielded inclusive results. The authors used rigorous criteria based on statistical analysis of the effects of several studies, and they used standard deviation as a process for comparing the results of several articles. After the authors reviewed and consolidated the results of 33 studies that used the instruments associated with the LMX and the TMX theories, they concluded that it was still unclear which of the constructs belonging to the two theories had more influence on workplace outcomes.

Banks et al. (2014) stated that employees do not know whether to invest time developing a relationship with their supervisor or with their team members. Furthermore, the authors noted that between the use of the LMX theory and the TMX theory, no study reported better social outcomes. The authors recommended that future research compare the impact of the constructs of both theories in the workplace. Banks et al. reiterated that while the LMX theory focuses on the vertical, supervisor-subordinate relationships, the TMX theory concentrates on the horizontal relationships between team members. Banks et al. suggested that due to employees' limited time resources, it is not clear if it is better for that employee to expand the vertical or the horizontal relationships.

Banks et al. (2014) argued that the results of the studies using the LMX and the TMX theories indicated that the two theories are incompatible. Banks et al. (2014) said that the theoretical framework of the LMX is the relationships between supervisors and subordinates. According to the LMX theory, a supervisor could grant or deny the resources to subordinates, and one of the constructs is negotiation. Researchers use the construct of the TMX to measure the quality of reciprocity among team members. The authors hypothesized there is a positive correlation between the LMX constructs and the TMX constructs.

Recent research by Bornay-Barrachina and Herrero (2018) examined workplace dynamics using the TMX theory. Bornay-Barrachina and Herrero (2018) conducted qualitative research to determine whether dual coworker relationships were significantly related to team performance. The authors investigated the dyadic coworker relationship in team performance. They recruited and interviewed 410 individuals belonging to 81 research and development teams in technology science research laboratories in a European country.

Bornay-Barrachina and Herrero (2018) hypothesized that the number of coworker interactions would be positively correlated with team performance. Additionally, the authors predicted that the quality of relationships among team members had a direct impact on the achievement of a team. With high regard for dual coworker relationships, Bornay-Barrachina and Herrero argued that team member relationships are still poorly understood as the investigation of dual coworker relationships is rare and uncommon. The authors asserted that the complexity of team interactions and the density of communication could cause high or low-quality communication among team members. Bornay-Barrachina and Herrero found that interaction significantly influenced the performance of the team members, but a team leader's impact was less influential on team members' performance. The authors reported that cooperation among team members was independent of the role of their leader. Additionally, Bornay-Barrachina and Herrero noted that team members' interactions were reciprocal.

Chun et al. (2016) investigated employee performance through the LMX and the TMX theories. The authors intended to illustrate the salient linkage of the LMX and the TMX relationships within teams. Additionally, Chun et al. wanted to study an individual team member's responsibility and desire to cooperate with the other team members. Chun et al. hypothesized that reciprocity-exchange of ideas and mutual assistance affected the performance of an entire team. Chun et al.'s analysis indicated that reciprocity was a vital process within team social interactions.

Chun et al. (2016) observed that recognition and feedback among team members manifested through reciprocity. Chun et al. reported a significant positive association between the constructs of the LMX and team performance. However, the result of this research did not produce a positive result between LMX constructs and knowledge sharing. The authors concluded that social interaction is the basis of reciprocity.

Huang et al. (2017) used the LMX and the TMX to explore the effects of organizational culture and social interaction on productivity. Huang et al. found a significant relationship between organizational culture and team social interactions and productivity. The authors determined the usefulness of the LMX constructs for describing the relationships between managers and employees. Huang et al. used the TMX constructs to measure the relationships between team members. Huang et al. reported that responsiveness and mutual sharing of knowledge are vital to project success. Furthermore, the authors claimed that shared mental models among team members for conducting corporate business would enhance mutual sharing of knowledge. Huang et al. claimed that mutual assistance improved the outcomes of a business unit and that social interaction between team members reduced misunderstandings.

T. Wu et al. (2014) used the LMX constructs and a trickle-down model to discover if the amount of nonwork support provided by high-level managers influenced the amount of nonwork support mid-level supervisors provided to employees. T. Wu et al. asserted that when mid-level managers receive nonwork support (i.e., the support provided outside of the workplace) from high-level managers, the mid-level managers provide similar support to their employees. T. Wu et al. (2014) conducted a survey and invited 200 participants to respond to their questionnaire. The authors received 184 responses from subordinates and 135 responses from supervisors. Fifty percent of the respondents were women, and participants' average length of employment was 10.32 years.

T. Wu et al. (2014) used a seven-point Likert scale ranging from 1 = *strongly disagree* to 7 = *strongly agree*. Their purpose was to examine the quality of their collected data and identify problems with the instrument. They examined the validity of their questionnaire using Cronbach's alpha, and the results were .94 for subordinates and .93 for supervisors. These results indicate that the instrument used by T. Wu et al. was valid and reliable. The review of T. Wu et al.'s study concludes this review of the literature on the LMX and the TMX. The next section addresses research focused on IT governance.

IT Governance

There have been several different avenues of research investigating the role of IT governance. Some researchers have focused on the administrative role of IT governance (Altemimi & Mohamad, 2015; Benaroch & Chernobai, 2017; Dawson, Denford, Williams, Preston, & Desouza, 2016; Shelly et al., 2015; Selig, 2016; Shelly et al., 2015). Other researchers have focused on the technical aspects of providing an appropriate environment for software developers to design and build software applications (Lunardi, Gastaud Maçada, Becker, & Van Grembergen, 2017; Nicho & Khan, 2017). What follows is a review of the literature addressing the aspects of the administrative role of IT governance that could coincide with the result of this research. The first article for IT governance was by Altemimi and Mohamad (2015).

Altemimi and Mohamad (2015) conducted a literature review about the vital role of IT governance. The authors reported numerous definitions of IT governance in the literature. Following their review of the literature, Altemimi and Mohamad suggested a model that could be used to explain IT governance. Altemimi and Mohamad's model was called the effective ITG landscape. Altemimi and Mohamad claimed that their model could assist managers in developing a better understanding of the role of IT governance.

Benaroch and Chernobai (2017) also researched the role of IT governance. Benaroch and Chernobai explored the direct link between the administrative role of IT governance and the failure of IT projects. The authors drew on the agency and resource dependency theory.

Benaroch and Chernobai claimed that the failure of IT projects was due to inadequate control by IT governance. The researchers hypothesized that there was a correlation between

IT project outcomes and the level of IT experience of IT governance board members.

To test their hypothesis, Benaroch and Chernobai (2017) collected data from 110 failed IT projects at public financial firms in the United States. The authors claimed that on average, the announcement of an IT project failure caused a firm to lose 1 billion dollars in equity value during the 4-day period following the announcement. Benaroch and Chernobai claimed that a link existed between the inadequacy of the IT experience of IT governance personnel and IT project failure. The authors asserted that their data supported the need for changes to IT governance. Benaroch and Chernobai recommended improving the level of IT competence and recruiting members with IT experience. The authors argued there was a link between enhanced IT board member competence and the reduction in failures of IT projects.

Benaroch and Chernobai (2017) subscribed to the idea that IT governance is responsible for the design and implementation of IT structures and procedures. Furthermore, the authors indicated that IT governance should screen IT functions to avoid project failure and ineffective use of IT assets. The authors indicated that selecting IT governance members with IT experience improves the probability of IT project success. Benaroch and Chernobai concluded that when IT governance fails to provide the proper software devolvement environment, IT project failure increases. Dawson et al. (2016) authored the next article in this IT governance review.

Dawson et al. (2016) used the agency theory to describe the role of IT governance in the public sector. The authors subscribed to the main hypothesis of the agency theory that an agent's actions are in full harmony with the objectives of the principal. Subsequently, the IT department of a company should implement the objectives set by the IT governance personnel. Dawson et al. described IT governance is the principal and the IT department as the agent. Within either sector, the authors said that IT governance is responsible for implementing the corporate strategic objectives or the public agency objectives. However, for the public sector and due to the political agenda of the elected officials, an agent's actions could contradict the objectives of the principal.

Based on their findings, Dawson et al. (2016) claimed that the agency theory is more applicable to the private sector than the public sector. Dawson et al. suggested more research regarding the extent of the relationship between the state legislature and IT governance regarding the funding of IT projects. The authors promoted the need for a new academic investigation of the role of IT governance in the public sector.

Dawson et al. (2016) noted that the role and accountability of IT governance vary considerably due to a wide range of definitions used by scholars and practitioners. In the private sector, Dawson et al. explained that IT governance is concerned with the utilization of IT to satisfy the immediate and future needs of an organization and its customers. Drawing on the agency theory, Dawson et al. characterized IT governance as the principal and IT staff as the agent. IT governance is responsible for providing financial incentives to the IT staff so that the staff can, in turn, provide effective and profitable IT services.

Dawson et al. (2016) claimed that in the private sector, the role of IT governance is to certify that IT department services do not deviate from the interests of the corporation. However, in the public sector, Dawson et al. noted that the goal of profit maximization is absent. The authors attributed the lack of profit enhancement to competing goals among politicians. Within either sector, IT governance is responsible for resource allocation, and often resources must be allocated to multiple competing IT projects. Dawson et al. noted that within both sectors, IT governance bodies occupy administrative roles.

Shelly et al. (2015) observed that previous studies characterized the role of IT governance differently. The authors acknowledged the vital role of previous research; however, they claimed that the strategic role of IT governance remains unclear. Shelly et al. conducted a survey and collected data in an attempt to clarify the role of IT governance in the context of organizational strategy. Their participants were executives and top-level managers working at 131 Taiwanese companies. Based on their findings, Shelly et al. asserted that the role of IT governance has a direct impact on a corporation's performance. To test their hypobook, Shelly et al. (2015) created a nomological network chart to indicate the role of IT governance. Their chart combined social setting and organizational performance. The authors claimed that their nomological network chart could create a shared understanding of the role of IT governance members in assisting top executives as they promoted IT-business alignment.

Selig (2016) conducted a historical narrative analysis of articles that promoted the creation of IT governance. After reviewing peer-reviewed articles and textbooks, the author suggested a plan for creating IT governance. Selig's plan identified the necessary characteristics and qualifications of IT governance members. These characteristics included leadership, flexibility, and the ability to create a suitable environment to harness technology. The plan included aspects related to both corporate business strategy and IT functions. Selig argued that

IT governance should be tasked with coordinating and carrying out an organization's plans. Additionally, Selig suggested that IT governance members should monitor IT department performance and IT outsourcing services and manage and develop IT staff. Selig promoted the IT governance role as a centralized management unit for controlling all the IT projects within a corporation.

Selig (2016) focused on the administrative role and explicit knowledge sharing among software developers. However, Selig did not elaborate on the IT governance members' qualifications. Selig suggested that corporations need to create a program management office as a center to coordinate and train software developers under the guidance of IT governance personnel. Selig emphasized that the essential role of IT governance is to manage different projects and improve cost-effectiveness ratios. Selig stated that meetings among software developers are crucial for the development of successful applications. Selig did not specifically address interactions between IT governance members and software developers. Selig also did not investigate the relationships between negotiation, reciprocity-exchange of ideas, reciprocitymeetings, and reciprocity-cohesiveness and knowledge sharing. The present study addressed that gap in the literature.

Negotiation

Software companies do not publish their negotiation processes nor the results of the negotiation between IT governance personnel and software teams. Therefore, there is a distinct lack of literature on the subject. Examining the processes of negotiation in other disciplines is an alternative way of measuring the usefulness of negotiation among software developers (Cook & Steinert, 2013). The literature review indicated a gap in what was known about the negotiation process between IT governance personnel and software developers. What follows is a review of research on the negotiation process by scholars such as Lehto (2015), Açıkgöz and Günsel (2016), Granatyr et al. (2015), and Busch and Henriksen (2018).

Lehto (2015) addressed negotiation among salespeople. Lehto (2015) noted that a successful negotiation necessitates prior training before engaging in an actual negotiation process. Lehto stated that negotiators usually try to resolve conflicts via the development of potential options that induce an acceptable alternative. Lehto (2015) noted that trust among negotiators is crucial for compromising and reaching an acceptable resolution that may arise from many different potential solutions.

Açıkgöz and Günsel (2016) investigated the decision process among engineering development teams and the role of individual creativity in discussion and negotiation. The authors stated that effective negotiation is characterized by continuing discussions among the members of a software engineering team. During an effective negotiation process, software developers reciprocally share information, assisting each other and volunteering to do extra work. Açıkgöz and Günsel (2016) claimed that the software teams that engaged in free discussion and negotiation expanded their skills and improved both group and individual performance.

Açıkgöz and Günsel (2016) found that individual creativity also had an impact on the decision-making process. Açıkgöz and Günsel (2016) claimed that software development teams could use decision-process models to aid in decision-making. The authors identified three creativity models: the interactionist model, the componential model, and the foundational model. The authors introduced their creativity model for software developers. The authors hypothesized that positive relationships existed between team decision processes, including negotiation, and successful software development.

Granatyr et al. (2015) conducted a literature review and examined social interactions among engineers to understand the decision-making process when conflicting suggestions are proposed. Granatyr et al. (2015) concluded that trust among the team members was instrumental in facilitating the selection of the appropriate solution to a problem. Granatyr et al. also found that honest conflict interactions enhanced trust. Granatyr et al. (2015) argued that trust facilitates the negotiation process and eases social interactions within teams dealing with conflict. Granatyr et al. (2015) noted that the agreed-on solutions are usually a consolidation of diverse, conflicting suggestions that must be defended by the engineering team members before being selected as a final decision. Granatyr et al. (2015) indicated that final decisions are influenced by the reputation, capabilities, honesty, and reliability of the engineers who submit the options.

The extent of the gap between two different views determines the complexity of the negotiation that must occur for parties to agree. The negotiation process is one way to reduce that gap (Busch & Henriksen, 2018). Busch and Henriksen (2018) investigated the nature of the negotiation process between government policymakers and government employees. The authors cautioned against the discretion that relates to making a judgment call. This discretion is a potential problem when agreed-upon terms govern a negotiation process. Discretion could allow an employee to act in ways that were not intended (Busch & Henriksen, 2018). Personal discretion and unilateral action can, in turn, impair trust, a factor that then makes further negotiation difficult.

Reciprocity

Seers (1989) developed the TMX theory, which included multiple constructs. One of these constructs was reciprocity. The literature review indicated that some researchers applied collective reciprocity as one construct while others divided the reciprocity construct into three district variables: reciprocity-exchange of ideas, reciprocity-meetings, and reciprocitycohesiveness. What follows is a review of the literature addressing the aspects of reciprocity that coincided with the objective of the present study. The next article for reciprocity review was by

Chen, Wei, and Xiaoguo Zhu (2018).

Chen et al. (2018) measured the constructs of reciprocity, peer recognition, and selfimage among users of an organized online community. The authors drew on their literature review to explain the relationships between the three constructs of reciprocity, peer recognition, and self-image. The authors sought to identify intrinsic and extrinsic motives that promote knowledge sharing among team members. Chen et al. used Bayesian estimation to measure the impact of motivation on knowledge sharing. Chen et al. claimed that motivation could elevate individuals from low levels of reciprocity to high levels. They reported that recognition and reputation could motivate employees to engage in reciprocal activities. Chen et al. (2018) noted that if users exchanged more information they also shared more knowledge. Chen et al. used the hidden Markov model to measure contribution and knowledge sharing among users (i.e., software developers). In contrast, this researcher adopted Nonaka's (1994) theory for explaining knowledge sharing among software developers.

> Schoenherr, Bendoly, Bachrach, and Hood (2017) studied reciprocity. Schoenherr et al.

found that in IT workgroups, individuals who provide technical assistance usually expect reciprocation when they require assistance. Schoenherr et al. explained that when a team member provides help but does not receive any in return, a nonequilibrium status develops. This lack of equilibrium within the group impairs further reciprocity between team members. Based on the inequity theory, Schoenherr et al. hypothesized that software developers who perceived they gave more technical assistance than they received would be more likely to adjust offers of help to other programmers in the future.

Schoenherr et al. collected data from 591 members in 107 implementation teams and found a statistically significant positive correlation between offering technical help and reciprocity for receiving technical support. Schoenherr et al. reported that when there was a gap between the help a software developer provided and the perceived help they received, that programmer reduced the future help they offered. The authors claimed that the magnitude of that gap could hinder the project success. The authors said that when a team member helps other members, the team member's assistance is usually a voluntary action. Based on the constructs of the inequity theory, the reduction in the future assistance is due to software developers' perceptions of their net gains from the interactions with other team members.

Schoenherr et al. (2017) cautioned that commissioning a team to design and build a software project does not automatically formulate teamwork. Schoenherr et al. noted conflict among IT team members regarding the inequity of reciprocity had not received proper attention in the scholarly literature. Schoenherr et al. reported that this research gap is especially apparent in the IT project literature. The authors suggested additional research should explore the inequity of reciprocity among software developers.

Schoenherr et al. (2017) claimed that interdependence characterizes the nature of software development tasks. Thus, the success or failure of an IT project is not entirely under the control of the most knowledgeable software developer or the least knowledgeable programmer on the same team. The authors theorized that the imbalance of the relationship between two software developers could lead to a reduction in the frequency of advice giving. The authors said that the nature of software development necessitates close cooperation and collaboration among team members.

Zhao, Detlor, and Connelly (2016) used the attribution theory and the theory of planned behavior to investigate the influence of extrinsic and intrinsic motivation on knowledge sharing and reciprocity. Zhao et al. related extrinsic motivation and its effect on intrinsic motivation to knowledge sharing among team members. Zhao et al. assembled several published instruments to create their survey. Participants included 968 people living in China with a minimum of one year of IT experience. Zhao et al. collected and analyzed data using structural equation modeling.

Zhao et al. (2016) predicted that knowledge sharing would flourish via reciprocity among team members. The authors explained that their study could offer insights for IT governance personnel on how to promote knowledge sharing via extrinsic and intrinsic motivations. Zhao et al. explained that intrinsic motivation would increase as a result of the enjoyment of helping other members of a team. A knowledge provider would feel contented by responding and explaining a complicated technical question to a receiver of knowledge. Additionally, knowledge providers would increase their expertise on a topic by explaining and assisting other team members.

Zhao et al. (2016) advocated promoting knowledge reciprocity among team members via extrinsic and intrinsic motivations. Furthermore, the authors posited that reciprocity among team members would increase expectations of further reciprocity. Zhao et al. noted that their investigation was significant in that it provided insight into the management of information systems. The review of Zhao et al. concluded reciprocity review section. Next is knowledge sharing review section.

Knowledge Sharing

While some researchers investigated knowledge sharing as a competitive advantage, or the learning and retention process, others studied knowledge sharing as a process for enhancing team performance. This section of the literature review addressed the aspects of knowledge sharing that coincided with the objectives of the current research. What follows first is a review of research conducted by Don-Jyh-Fu and Dunk (2013).

Don-Jyh-Fu and Dunk (2013) conducted a quantitative, nonexperimental study to determine if there was a correlation between knowledge sharing and the success of enterprise resource planning (ERP) installations. They used an online survey and recruited participants from North and South America. Their survey yielded 187 useable responses. The authors said that 13% of the surveyed companies reported very satisfactory results with the installation of ERP. Another 59% of companies reported overrun costs. In total, 93% of the respondents indicated that the installations took longer than expected. Don-Jyh-Fu and Dunk reported that the knowledge-sharing process provided a method for successful ERP installations and helped the participating companies retain competitive advantage. Don-Jyh-Fu and Dunk said that knowledge sharing among software developers assisted in the success of ERP installations.

In another study on knowledge sharing, Huang and Zhang (2016) investigated the association between individual activities and knowledge sharing among IT professionals in an online setting. The authors conducted their research using a "systems, applications, and products (SAP)" community network. The authors conducted a quantitative, nonexperimental study to explore the correlation between learning and retention. Huang and Zhang indicated that both intrinsic and extrinsic motives directly impacted knowledge sharing and learning among software developers.

Huang and Zhang (2016) tested two hypobook. First, they hypothesized that knowledge contributors have superior expertise, and second, they hypothesized that those who sought knowledge wanted to improve their job performance. Huang and Zhang claimed that their research provided empirical evidence that extrinsic and intrinsic motives improved job performance. The authors concluded that training was positively correlated with retention. Their analyses indicated that learning and knowledge acquisition reduced turnover. Furthermore, Huang and Zhang stated that management (i.e., IT governance) should be aware of intrinsic and extrinsic employee motives.

Ozer and Vogel (2015) conducted quantitative, nonexperimental research to find a correlation between received knowledge and performance. Additionally, they wanted to measure the influence of social interaction on knowledge sharing among software developers. Ozer and Vogel measured received knowledge as an independent variable and job performance as a dependent variable. The authors recommended that software developers should incorporate shared knowledge in new applications. Ozer and Vogel contended that shared knowledge is not usually incorporated in the design of a new application. Through a theoretical lens that combined the task closure theory, the social exchange theory, and the LMX theory, Ozer and Vogel described the interrelation between knowledge sharing and performance. Within the context of the task closure theory, when a team member applies received knowledge, it brings closure to the knowledge-sharing process.

Trantopoulos et al. (2017) investigated the influence of external knowledge and IT on knowledge absorption and innovation in a company. The authors adopted the knowledge-based view of the firm (KBV) theory to examine the conditions under which a firm augments external knowledge. Trantopoulos et al. believed that adopting a KBV could affect the performance of a firm. The authors developed a model to test their hypobook. Trantopoulos et al. collected data from Swiss firms that specialized in manufacturing over a 9-year period. Using a survey, the authors collected data from almost 3,500 Swiss manufacturing firms to measure the impact of external knowledge on innovation and the role of IT in facilitating knowledge distribution. The authors cited a need to create a process to capture new knowledge and disseminate it among employees. The authors argued that making information available to employees allows for efficient processes and production.

Carlsen (2016) conducted a narrative analysis to describe the role of employees in organizational knowledge sharing. Carlsen's research focused on tacit organizational identity and its impact on employees. Carlsen claimed that organizations have tacit identities, and a tacit organizational identity is based on employee narrations and external influence. Carlsen said that identifying an organizational identity is a difficult task, but corporations differentiate themselves for strategic competitive advantage. A tacit organizational identity is constructed through reflexivity and scrutiny of the organization's services and products.

Carlsen argued that surveys and interviews do not allow a researcher to understand a tacit organizational identity. The tacit identity of an organization is a collection of dynamic constructs formed from the interplay between internal and external elements (Carlsen, 2016). Carlsen concluded that the current research guidance for investigating tacit organizational identity is limited, and more investigation is warranted. Furthermore, Carlsen reported that a tacit organizational identity requires self-reflexive examination of unconscious assumptions that may or may not to be true. Carlsen stated that tacit organizational identity research is a link between empirical observations and theories.

Carlsen (2016) gave an overview of the nature of a tacit organizational identity via empirical observations and theories. The author indicated that there are three pillars of a tacit organizational identity: (a) self-as-object, (b) self-as-subject, and (c) self-as-stories. Carlsen noted that the primary goal of the research was to establish a tool to understand the formation of an organization's tacit identity. This understanding could, in turn, shed light on assumptions about tacit roles in organizations.

Davern, Shaft, and Te'eni (2012) investigated software development and the impact of cognitive qualities on cooperativity among team members to better understand knowledge sharing in team settings. Davern et al. wanted to find out about the effect of cognitive qualities on cooperativity among team members. The authors conducted a historical narrative analysis of articles on the role of cognition among software developers. The authors defined cognition as knowing and the use of knowledge.

Davern et al. (2012) found that information system development depends on perceptions, and understating the role of cognition would impact software development. The authors illustrated their claim via a flow chart, which was an external representation of a mental model that software developers use to develop an application. Davern et al. claimed that mental models help software developers communicate effectively. These models, Davern et al. noted, are practical tools for communication, and developers use models to discover anomalies in program design or to identify alternative designs. The authors suggested that creating a software system is a mental process, and designers visualize the system before writing programs. Flowcharts are an example of the mental imaging designers utilize when creating an application. Davern et al. stated that IT governance personnel should encourage software developers to create charts and let other team members evaluate the charts.

Mangalaraj et al. (2014) conducted a qualitative study to investigate the challenges of social interaction among software developers. They focused on cognitive systems and the challenges of designing successful software applications.

Mangalaraj et al. concluded that close social interaction among team members and paired software designers produced better results than working individually. Additionally, Mangalaraj et al. indicated that designing and building a successful software application is very knowledge intensive, and it requires selecting a solution from a large number of alternatives.

Mangalaraj et al. (2014) claimed there is a need to investigate social interactions among software developers by pairing an expert with a novice. The authors reported that the exchange of information among team members could lead to improved problem-solving. Mangalaraj et al. noted that teams engaged in intensive interaction produced better results than teams that had limited communication. Despite the required intensive interaction and exploration of different team cognitions, the authors reported that very few researchers investigated the role of cognition in software development. Furthermore, Mangalaraj et al. hypothesized that collaborating team members produced better results than individuals. The review of Mangalaraj et al.'s research concludes the literature review section. The next section contains a synthesis of the research findings.

Synthesis of the Research Findings

The primary objective of a synthesis of research is to combine diverse articles into a comprehensive and logical assessment. Furthermore, the researcher reported the strengths and the weaknesses of the reviewed articles. The researcher investigated the role of IT governance (i.e., negotiation) and reciprocity (i.e., exchange of ideas, meetings, and cohesiveness) among software team members. The literature review indicated that some researchers drew on the LMX theory as the theoretical foundation of their studies, while other investigators subscribed to the TMX theory or Nonaka's (1994) knowledge-sharing theory. Despite the use of different theories, these researchers sought to describe how social exchange and interactions among people influenced the success of IT teams and projects. The following sections synthesize articles that relied on the LMX theory and the TMX theory when investigating IT governance, negotiation, reciprocity. A final section address knowledge-sharing in the context of Nonaka's knowledgesharing theory.

LMX Synbook

While some researchers used the LMX theory as the theoretical foundation of their studies, they did not describe the theory's constructs adequately. For example, Windeler and Riemenschneider (2016) utilized the LMX theory to define and understand the social exchange relationships between minority IT software developers and their supervisors. Windeler and

Riemenschneider, however, failed to describe the LMX theory and its four constructs adequately. Additionally, Zagenczyk, Purvis, Shoss, Scott, and Cruz (2015) subscribed to the LMX theory to explore and report on the emotional support and exchange of resources between employees and their supervisors. Zagenczyk et al. (2015) also failed to describe the four basic constructs of the LMX. Liu, Song, Li, and Liao (2017) stated that they used the LMX theory, but the authors did not offer a description or an explanation of the LMX theory. Furthermore, Gutermann, LehmannWillenbrock, Boer, Born, and Voelpel (2017) also drew on the LMX theory without adequately explaining the theory's constructs.

When developing the LMX theory, Dansereau et al. (1975) described the four constructs of the LMX theory as negotiating latitude, a superior's contribution, a member's contribution, and outcomes. The lack of explanation and justification for the use of the LMX theory based on these constructs was common among the studies by Gutermann et al. (2017), Liu et al. (2017), Windeler and Riemenschneider (2016), and Zagenczyk et al. (2015). Readers who are not familiar with the rationale of the development of the LMX, as explained in Dansereau et al.

(1975), would not be able to interpret the context and implications of these studies effectively.

TMX Synbook

While some researchers subscribed to the TMX theory and used its constructs to investigate the social exchange interactions among employees, the topic of their studies varied extensively. Farmer et al. (2015) drew on the TMX theory and organizational citizenship behavior (OCB) to examine the personal relationships between team members. Farmer et al. suggested that high-quality TMX relationships would lead to a sense of belonging. That feeling of belonging and the identification with a group, in turn, improves the quality of the interactions between team members.

Farmer et al. (2015) predicted that high-quality interactions between team members would result in higher levels of identification with coworkers. Farmer et al. also reported a link between higher levels of team identification and higher levels of team performance. Due to the small amount of previous empirical studies, Farmer et al. called for more research on the horizontal relationships between team members. Farmer et al. suggested that researchers specifically focus on the link between these horizontal relationships and task accomplishments such as software development.

Farh, Lanaj, and Ilies (2017) investigated individual team performance and mutual obligations of social exchange relationships. Specifically, Farh et al. studied the interactions between help providers and help receivers. Farh et al. found that one critical aspect of dyadic social exchange relationships between co-workers was the feeling of obligation to return the favor once a colleague or a team member had provided help.

Liao, Yang, Wang, Drown, and Shi (2013) also used the constructs of the TMX with their study. Liao et al. investigated employees' role in teamwork and team performance. The authors examined social exchanges between team members to determine whether individual performance could be improved through group-based accomplishment. Liao et al. addressed the impact of team members' different personality traits on the TMX constructs. Liao et al. claimed that the data indicated personality traits did impact team performance.

Schermuly and Meyer (2016) used the constructs of the TMX to investigate the psychological health of employees. Schermuly and Meyer found that social relationships could affect the health status of an employee. Schermuly and Meyer drew on the constructs of the

TMX to measure the impact of co-worker interactions on an employee's psychological health. Schermuly and Meyer argued that direct social exchange with other team members could empower an employee. The authors reported that follower-follower direct social exchange relationships helped employees deal with stress. Furthermore, the authors advocated that management (i.e., IT governance) should focus on preventing conflict escalation, which could increase the level of depression among employees.

IT Governance Synbook

There have been several different avenues of research into IT governance. This section synthesizes the articles reviewed during this study. Examples of recent research on IT governance include studies by Altemimi and Mohamad (2015), Benaroch and Chernobai (2017), Shelly et al. (2015), and Selig (2016).

Altemimi and Mohamad (2015) conducted a literature review of articles on the role of IT governance and found that scholars define IT governance in different ways. As a result, the authors concluded that the role of IT governance remains unclear. Altemimi and Mohamad developed a model that they claimed could improve the role of IT governance and increase the return on investments. However, the authors did not elaborate on how their model could cut the cost of IT projects. Additionally, Altemimi and Mohamad claimed that adopting tools such as Control Objectives for Information and Related Technologies (COBIT) and Information Technology

Infrastructure Library (ITIL) could improve IT project success rates. The authors did not provide evidence supporting their claim. Altemimi and Mohamad (2015) indicated that one of their goals was to promote the administrative role of IT governance.

Benaroch and Chernobai (2017) investigated the connection between the administrative role of IT governance and the failure of IT projects. The authors claimed that the result of their data analyses provided evidence of an association between the experience levels of IT governance personnel and IT project failure. Benaroch and Chernobai argued that enhancing the IT competency of the IT governance board members could reduce the failure of IT projects.

Shelly et al. (2015) claimed that previous research provided different perspectives on the role of IT governance. Shelly et al. acknowledged that scholars had conducted a great deal of research; however, they claimed that the strategic role of IT governance remained unclear. Shelly et al. claimed that the role of IT governance has a direct impact on a corporation's performance, but they did not provide evidence supporting their claim. Furthermore, the authors acknowledged that a link exists between an organization's strategic objectives and the duties of the IT department.

Selig (2016) addressed the role of IT governance and explained the different administrative functions of IT governance. The author noted the essential role of IT governance in managing different projects and improving cost-effectiveness ratios. Selig did not address the importance of interactions between software team members, nor did Selig investigate the collective impact of negotiation, reciprocity-exchange of ideas, reciprocity-meetings, and reciprocity-cohesionless on knowledge sharing.

Negotiation Synthesis

Many findings emerged from the research on negotiation. While some researchers focused on the general negotiation process between IT governance and employees, another critical aspect of negotiation is its impact on individual creativity (Açıkgöz & Günsel, 2016). Lehto (2015) advocated that successful negotiation processes require prior training before engaging in actual negotiation interactions. Açıkgöz and Günsel (2016) claimed that teams that participated in free discussion and negotiation expanded the skills and the performance of the team members.

Granatyr et al. (2015) advocated that trust would facilitate the negotiation process and ease social interactions when building agreements between IT governance personnel and IT development teams. Busch and Henriksen (2018) investigated the nature of the negotiation process between government policymakers and government employees. The research indicated that negotiation processes are similar in both the public and the private sector. The present researcher studied the negotiation process between supervisors and subordinates in the private sector. Contrary to the four peer-reviewed articles examined in this literature review, the present researcher explicitly adopted the LMX theory with its negotiation construct as a measurement.

Reciprocity Synbook

Researchers investigated the impact of reciprocity among IT software developers and team members from different perspectives regarding knowledge sharing. Chen et al. (2018), Park and Lee (2014), Schoenherr et al. (2017), and Zhao et al. (2016) all investigated the impact of reciprocity in different social exchange settings. For example, Chen et al. (2018) focused on the cause of reciprocity. Chen et al. (2018) measured the constructs of reciprocity, peer recognition, and self-image among users of an online community. The authors were interested in identifying the elements that cause reciprocity among team members due to intrinsic and extrinsic motives. Park and Lee (2014) were not interested in identifying the cause of reciprocity. Instead, they were interested in measuring the impact of trust on reciprocity. Park and Lee investigated the relationship between trust and reciprocity among programmers. The authors reported that reciprocity would flourish based if the team members trusted one another.

Schoenherr et al. (2017) reported that when working in teams, IT professionals who provide technical assistance to other team members expect a reciprocal action from the team member that receives help. Schoenherr et al. found that if help was not reciprocated, a nonequilibrium status would develop within the team, and the lack of equilibrium would, in turn, reduce future offers of assistance. Schoenherr et al. hypothesized that software developers who perceived they gave more technical assistance than they received would begin to offer less help to other programmers in the team. Schoenherr et al. (2017) argued that reciprocity among software team members had not received an adequate amount of attention from scholars.

Chen et al. (2018) investigated the intrinsic and extrinsic motives for reciprocity. In similar research, Zhao et al. (2016) investigated the influence of extrinsic motivations on intrinsic motivations to reciprocate. These scholars wanted to determine whether knowledge sharing would increase via reciprocity among team members. Zhao et al. hypothesized that knowledge providers would feel more competent when they shared knowledge and explained information to other team members.

Knowledge-Sharing Synbook

The research on knowledge sharing is diverse. While some researchers focused on finding a correlation between software developers' knowledge sharing and the success of enterprise resource planning implementation (Don-Jyh-Fu & Dunk, 2013), others concentrated on learning and retention of the knowledge shared by software developers (Huang & Zhang, 2016). Researchers also investigated a correlation between knowledge receiving and the performance (Açıkgöz & Günsel, 2016) of the receiver's knowledge (Ozer & Vogel, 2015). Trantopoulos et al. (2017) examined the influence of external knowledge on knowledge absorption and innovation in a company.

Carlsen (2016) reported that sharing information on employees' past technical experiences was an indication of the future team interactions. Carlson found that individuals would reciprocate if other team members shared their professional knowledge and expertise.

Carlsen claimed that cooperation among team members would lead to increased collaboration.

Furthermore, Carlsen argued that an organizational culture that promoted team knowledgesharing would increase knowledge transfer. The following section provides a critique of the methods used to conduct the research in this literature review.

Critique of Previous Research Methods

While some researchers focused on knowledge sharing in general and identified their target populations, other authors did not adequately identify the target population, sample frame, or sample (Farh et al., 2017; Kilic, 2018; Zagenczyk et al., 2015). Thus, a researcher faces a challenging task to critique an article that provides information on neither the sample frame nor the population. What follows first is a section about LMX articles, second TMX articles, followed by IT governance articles, negotiation articles and then reciprocity articles, and finally, knowledge-sharing articles.

Critique of the LMX

Windeler and Riemenschneider (2016) invited 554 IT workers from a Fortune 500 company to participate in their research. A total of 289 IT workers agreed to participate. The authors adopted the LMX theory to study career mentoring among minority IT software programmers. However, the authors did not indicate how many minority programmers were among the 289 IT workers that agreed to participate in the study. When referencing the LMX, Windeler and Riemenschneider often neglected to indicate whether they were referring to the LMX theory or the 7-item LMX instrument. Windeler and Riemenschneider indicated that they used a 7-point, Likert scale when they should have described the scale as a Likert-type scale (Sullivan & Artino, 2013). Windeler and Riemenschneider also failed to clearly describe their research method, which made replication of the study impossible. These issues impaired the credibility of Windeler and Riemenschneider's findings.

Zagenczyk et al. (2015) failed to reference the sample frame or their target population when reporting the results of their research. Zagenczyk et al. provided their study participants with a questionnaire, and in exchange for their participation, the researchers provided each respondent with a box lunch and a cash payment. This approach to data collection had the potential to cause apprehension and fear among some participants who could be afraid to reveal their honest opinions when directly interacting with the researchers. This approach also may have led some individuals to complete the questionnaire based on a desire to obtain the cash payment instead of out of a desire to contribute to a better understanding of the study topic.

Liu et al. (2017) used the term LMX to refer to a set of constructs, which could lead to confusion among individuals unfamiliar with the LMX theory. Liu et al. (2017) implied that they used an instrument for collecting their data; however, they did not report the name of their instrument. A researcher experienced with the LMX theory and the 7-item LMX instrument could extrapolate that the authors used the instrument from the LMX theory. However, without confirmation, the study was not replicable. Liu et al. developed a mobile, handheld piece of software that was installed on each participant's mobile phone. Unfortunately, Liu et al. failed to provide evidence of the accuracy of that software, a fact that could have compromised the integrity of their collected data (Sekaran & Bougie, 2014). Finally, Liu et al. potentially influenced their participants by providing cash and lotteries as enticements for their participation.

Gutermann et al. (2017) indicated that they collected data from teams who worked for a company in Germany. Each team reported to one supervisor, but the members of each team worked independently. The company adopted a hierarchical structure. Gutermann et al.

translated the LMX items into German using two bilingual translators. The reader could not determine whether they translated the entire LMX theory text or if they translated only the seven items of the LMX instrument. One problem with their measurement was directing the participants to recall from memory their evaluations from the previous year's annual performance assessments. Responding to survey items based on memory can lead to inconsistent responses (Sekaran & Bougie, 2014).

Gutermann et al. (2017), Liu et al. (2017), Windeler and Riemenschneider (2016), and

Zagenczyk et al. (2015) mixed ordinal scales and Likert scales. According to Sekaran and Bougie (2014), researchers use ordinal scales to let the participants determine their preferences for a sequence of choices. Thus, when using ordinal scales, participants rank their choices from the low end of a scale to the high end of a scale. Field (2013) used silver, bronze, and gold as an example of items that could be placed in an ordinal scale; the ordinal scale would be 1 = bronze, 2 = silver, and 3 = gold. While many researchers refer to their instruments as Likert scales,

Likert scales are not true ordinal scales. Gutermann et al. (2017), Windeler and Riemenschneider (2016), Liu et al. (2017), and Zagenczyk et al. (2015) indicated they used a 7-point Likert scale when they should have stated that they used a Likert-type scale (Sullivan & Artino, 2013).

TMX Critique

When reviewing the research by Liao et al. (2013), there was a concern over the authors' data collection processes. Liao et al. claimed they surveyed participants anonymously, but the participants were allowed to respond to the questionnaires either during the working hours or after work. This process could have been scrutinized to determine which responses were attributable to which participants. Additionally, Liao et al. translated the questionnaire from English to Chinese and then back to English. That translation could compromise the intended meaning of the original English instrument. Furthermore, Liao et al. recruited participants who provided labor to load and unload pallets. Thus, Liao et al.'s findings may not closely relate to research using the constructs of the TMX to measure knowledge sharing among software developers.

When studying the TMX theory, Farh et al. (2017) focused on the collective impact of reciprocity. In contrast, the present research addressed the three subconstructs of reciprocity.

This researcher decomposed the TMX construct of reciprocity into three subconstructs:

reciprocity-exchange of ideas, reciprocity-meetings, and reciprocity-cohesiveness. In contrast to Farh et al., the present study used a Liker-type scale for data collection instead of a strict Likert scale. A novice reader would have difficulty identifying the research method Farh et al. used.

Additionally, Farh et al. indicated that they used only 10 items of the instrument that Seers (1989) developed without explicitly mentioning which 10 items they had selected from the 34- item instrument. Thus, a researcher that would like to replicate Farh et al.'s research would have some difficulty.

Farh et al. (2017) directly reported their research sample without indicating either the sample frame or the target population. They selected 236 participants working for a large multinational bank in Singapore. One alarming element of Farh et al.'s research was the lack of confidentiality during data collection. Participants completed the surveys in group meetings.

These concerns limited the applicability of Farh et al.'s research to other populations.

In other research on the TMX, Farmer et al. (2015) unintentionally failed to ensure there was a common link between the supervisors and the subordinates in their study. Farmer et al. used the OCB to collect data from the supervisors and the TMX instrument for collecting data from the employees. The supervisors rated their employees and the employees rated each other without describing an intersection between the two sets of data. Farmer et al. also failed to provide the names of the instruments they used to collect data. Finally, Farmer et al.

inappropriately referred to their instruments as being Likert-scaled instead of a Likert-type scale.

In a final example of flawed research on the TMX, Schermuly and Meyer (2016) acknowledged that they did not test whether the constructs of the LMX were stronger than the constructs of the TMX. Furthermore, Schermuly and Meyer did not address the subconstructs of reciprocity, which limits comparability with the present study. Schermuly and Meyer also failed to report the names of the instruments they used to collect data. Thus, an investigator interested in repeating their investigation would face a problem in finding the instrument they used to collect their data.

IT Governance Critique

Selig (2016) noted that meetings among software developers are crucial for the development of successful applications, yet the author did not cover the technical interaction between IT governance members and software developers. Selig did not collect empirical data, and instead provided a consolidated review of the role of IT governance by conducting a literature review. Selig failed to indicate the range of years for the articles in his review. Selig utilized ITIL, an integrated tool for managing the design and implementation of a software application. This decision limited the generalizability of Selig's findings.

Altemimi and Mohamad (2015) relied extensively on the usage of COBIT and ITIL as tools to assist IT governance in managing software developments. Altemimi and Mohamad claimed that the IT governance framework they articulated for the creation of rules and control could improve project success rates. They focused on the administrative role of IT governance and disregarded the technical role of IT governance. Altemimi and Mohamad elaborated on the structure of their suggested IT governance model without referencing software developers.

Furthermore, their list of references included articles that dealt primarily with the management aspects of IT governance excluding articles that dealt with the technical role of IT governance.

Shelly et al. (2015) addressed the role of IT governance from an administrative perspective. Shelly et al. conducted a survey and collected data from executives and high-level employees in Taiwanese companies. Shelly et al. did not address the relationship between IT governance members and software developers. Instead, the authors focused on the strategic and administrative role of IT governance. Shelly et al. claimed that the relationship between IT governance and organizational performance is still unclear.

Benaroch and Chernobai (2017) indicated that they used Financial Institutions Risk Scenario Trends (FIRST) for their data. However, they failed to provide a full reference, and this researcher could not locate it. Benaroch and Chernobai focused on the financial role of IT governance, limiting the study's relevance to the technical, social exchange of ideas between IT governance members and software developers. Benaroch and Chernobai investigated the budget of IT governance in relation to total corporate investments. Thus, Benaroch and Chernobai's research was limited in its applicability to the relationships studied in the present study.

Negotiation Critique

Lehto (2015) conducted qualitative interviews with five Finnish entrepreneurs who had extended their business globally. The author contacted potential participants via telephone calls and met personally with the participants. Lehto (2015) only spent an hour collecting data from each participant via face-to-face interviews. The short duration of the data collection could hinder the viability and reliability of the results.

Açıkgöz and Günsel (2016) applied structural equation modeling (SEM) to analyze their study data. SEM requires more advanced statistical skills than a process like multiple linear regression analysis. However, the authors committed a mistake by writing Likert-scaled instead of the Likert-type scale. The authors indicated that they used a 5-point Likert scale ranging from

1 = *strongly disagree* to 5 = *strongly agree*. Instead, they should have written that they used a Likert-type scale (Sullivan

& Artino, 2013). According to Sekaran and Bougie (2014), researchers use ordinal scales to let the participants determine their preferences for a sequence of choices. Thus, with these types of scales, participants rank their selections from low to high.

However, sometimes these scales collect interval data rather than ordinal data.

Using a qualitative method, Granatyr et al. (2015) reviewed 230 articles covering trust and reputation among agents. Despite reviewing 230 articles, Granatyr et al. only included summaries for five of the articles they reviewed in their paper. Readers would have benefited from the classification of all the 230 papers into different categories. Additionally, Granatyr et al.

failed to clearly articulate the methods of the data collection used by the different researchers when synthesizing the five articles.

Busch and Henriksen (2018) conducted a literature review on digital discretion. They collected 251 peer-reviewed manuscripts, from which they selected 20 articles to review as part of their research. The authors indicated that the 20 articles covered public service employees. Busch and Henriksen did not review any research that covered digital discretion and private service employees. An expert would discover the inconstancy between the number of peerreviewed articles mentioned in their abstract (44) and the fact that only 20 articles were included in their final analyses.

Reciprocity Critique

Zhao et al. (2016) used a quantitative nonexperimental method for collecting data on reciprocity from participants via an online webpage. Unfortunately, Zhao et al. did not give the full name of the instrument. Chen et al. (2018) also used a quantitative nonexperimental structural model to identify the level of cooperation among team members. However, the authors did not sort the questions and responses according to their complexity. Instead, they used the Bayesian estimation of the model and reported low, medium, and high types of questions and responses. Users who raised issues determined the low, medium, and high evaluations. This approach meant that users that could not accurately assess the complexity of the questions might inadvertently give a low grade to the specialist even if the specialist had answered their complicated questions.

> Schoenherr et al. (2017) also studied reciprocity. Schoenherr et al. engaged the Project

Management Institute to assist in obtaining participants for their study. Unfortunately, Schoenherr et al. failed to disclose whether the participants were from the United States or whether the sample included individuals from many countries. Because the authors failed to report their target population and clarify geographically where the sample was located, the generalizability of their findings was limited.

Knowledge-Sharing Critique

Some researchers used quantitative methods while others adopted qualitative methods. For example, Don-Jyh-Fu and Dunk (2013) used instruments to collect quantitative data on knowledge sharing. Additionally, Huang and Zhang (2016) conducted quantitative nonexperimental research collecting data from software developers in an online open society supported by a vendor. Researchers should be aware of the influence of financial support from a vendor. To protect data integrity and the participants' identities, this researcher collected data from participants who were not under the control of a vendor and who participated anonymously. Ozer and Vogel (2015) collected data to measure the impact of knowledge sent about a receiver's performance. Ozer and Vogel claimed that software developers' direct contact would lead to common sharing experiences. Additionally, Ozer and Vogel did not investigate knowledge sharing among software developers through reciprocity-exchange of ideas, reciprocity-meetings, and, reciprocity-cohesiveness.

Trantopoulos et al. (2017) used three waves of surveys to collect data from European participants to measure the impact of external knowledge on innovation and knowledge sharing among employees. To measure the impact of external knowledge, Trantopoulos et al. designed their new instrument. In contrast, to collect data, this researcher used previously published instruments that measured the variables of negotiation (i.e., the LMX construct); reciprocity (i.e., the TMX construct); and knowledge sharing (Nonaka, 1994). Carlsen (2016) focused on research to develop a vocabulary describing knowledge sharing within corporations. Carlsen indicated that employees' association with their company promoted knowledge sharing. This researcher addressed knowledge sharing among software developers via the reciprocity construct from the

TMX theory.

Summary

Chapter 2 offered a review of the extant literature on software development knowledge sharing. Chapter 3 provides a detailed explanation of the research design including the purpose of the study, the research questions and hypobook, the research design, the target population and sample, the procedures followed during the study, and the data collection instrument.

Chapter 4 contains the results of the data analysis, and Chapter 5 summarizes the results and provides a conclusion to the study.

CHAPTER 3. Methodology Overview: Knowledge Sharing Study

The primary objective of this study was to examine negotiation and reciprocity related to knowledge sharing among software developers using a quantitative nonexperimental method. This investigation utilized multiple regression analyses to determine the relationship between the variables. This chapter identifies the methodology used to conduct the study. Chapter 3 begins with the purpose of the study and concludes a summary.

Purpose of the Study

The purpose of this research was to measure the effect of both IT governance and reciprocity on knowledge sharing in software development teams. The intent was to examine negotiation between IT governance leaders and software development team members to explore vertical knowledge-sharing relationships between supervisors and subordinates. The intent of examining reciprocity was to understand knowledge-sharing processes in the context of the horizontal exchange of ideas between peers (Buvik & Tvedt, 2017; Chun et al., 2016; Deng et al., 2017; Huang et al., 2017; Yoshikawa, 2017). The need to develop a clear understanding of knowledge sharing interactions among software developers was justified by Ozer and Vogel (2015) who indicated that investments in software development in the United States during 2015 exceeded 300 billion dollars. This topic is particularly important as the failure of IT projects was recently estimated at approximately $78 billion annually in the United States (Standish Group,

2014).

This quantitative nonexperimental study was designed to determine if there was a statistically significant association between perceived levels of negotiation between IT governance members and software developers and levels of knowledge sharing regarding software development. The study also addressed reciprocity between team members. This study investigated a gap in the literature regarding the effects of vertical negotiation between IT governance (e.g., team leaders, IT managers, and senior IT management) and software developers. Mainly, the investigation addressed whether the amount and frequency of negotiation between IT governance and software developers were associated with levels of knowledge sharing among software developers (see Bornay-Barrachina & Herrero, 2018; Sanders, 2014; Yau & Tan, 2017; Yukl, 2013). Additionally, this study was designed to examine whether the amount and frequency of reciprocity processes (i.e., reciprocity-exchange of ideas, reciprocity-meetings, and reciprocity-cohesiveness) among software developers were associated with the level of knowledge sharing that occurred between software development team members (see Cândido & Sousa, 2017; Takpuie & Tanner, 2016; Zhao et al., 2016).

To address knowledge gaps in the scholarly literature, this researcher evaluated two specific knowledge-sharing processes: (a) vertical knowledge sharing between IT governance personnel and software developers (see Sollitto et al., 2016) and (b) horizontal knowledge sharing between members of software development teams (see de Jong et al., 2014). This study had two independent variables and one dependent variable. The independent variables were negotiation and reciprocity. Reciprocity consisted of three subvariables: reciprocity-exchange of ideas, reciprocity-meetings, and reciprocity-cohesiveness. The dependent variable was knowledge sharing, defined as the amount and frequency of knowledge sharing among software developers.

The need for better understanding of the impacts of negotiation with IT governance and reciprocity between software developers was justified by Ozer and Vogel (2015) who noted the high failure rate of software development projects. Researchers have argued that the failure of IT projects was due to the lack of knowledge sharing among software developers (Colnar & Dimovski, 2017). The success of a project can be compromised when a team member has critical technical knowledge that can be hidden or hoarded from another team member that needs it (Connelly et al., 2012). For example, if software developers do not share knowledge, it can cause the same technical errors to be committed several times (Ozer & Vogel, 2015). Furthermore, Rezaei et al. (2017) argued that employees (e.g., software developers) need to have active channels of communication to achieve a common goal.

The research design and methodology are presented in this chapter. Chapter 3 begins with a presentation of the research questions and hypobook. The chapter also includes descriptions of the research design; the target population, sample, and power analysis; and procedures related to participant selection, the protection of participants, and data collection. Subsequently, Chapter 3 includes an overview of the specific descriptive statistics, hypothesis testing, and instruments used to analyze the data. The chapter concludes with a description of the instrument used to collect the data, a discussion of ethical considerations, and a summary.

Research Questions and Hypobook

Primary Research Question

Primary Research Question. To what extent do negotiation and reciprocity relate to knowledge sharing among software developers?

Research Subquestions

Research Subquestion 1. To what extent is the software developers' negotiation with IT governance related to knowledge sharing among team members? The researcher tested the following hypobook to answer this research question.

$H_0$1: Software developers' negotiation with IT governance is not significantly related to knowledge sharing among team members.

H_a1: Software developers' negotiation with IT governance is significantly related to knowledge sharing among team members.

Research Subquestion 2. To what extent are the reciprocity-exchange of ideas with other software developers related to knowledge sharing among team members?

$H_0 2$: The reciprocity-exchange of ideas with other software developers is not significantly related to knowledge sharing among team members.

$H_a 2$: The reciprocity-exchange of ideas with other software developers is significantly related to knowledge sharing among team members.

Research Subquestion 3. To what extent are the reciprocity-meetings with other software developers related to knowledge sharing among team members?

$H_0 3$: The reciprocity-meetings with other software developers are not significantly related to knowledge sharing among team members.

H_a3: The reciprocity-meetings with other software developers are significantly related to knowledge sharing among team members.

Research Subquestion 4. To what extent is reciprocity-cohesiveness of a software development team related to knowledge sharing among software development team members?

H₀4: The reciprocity-cohesiveness of software developing team is not significantly related to knowledge sharing among team members.

H_a4: The reciprocity-cohesiveness of software developing team is significantly related to knowledge sharing among team members.

Research Design

This researcher used a quantitative, nonexperimental research design for the present study because a post hoc method did not allow for direct manipulation of experimental variables (Schiavo, Cappelletti, Mencarini, Stock, &

Zancanaro, 2016). With the chosen method, there was only one group of participants. A quantitative, nonexperimental approach does not use controlled and uncontrolled units for comparisons (Deaton & Cartwright, 2017). This researcher applied a quantitative, nonexperimental design because there was no control group exposed to certain conditions or treatments.

According to van Asseldonk, Lans, and Kleijer (2017), an advantage of using a quantitative nonexperimental approach is that it allows a researcher to test the impact of independent variables on a dependent variable. In the present study, the researcher tested the influence of negotiation and reciprocity on software developers' knowledge sharing. The cost of acquiring the necessary data using a quantitative nonexperimental design is far less than that of an experimental approach because the former does need multiple groups (Deaton & Cartwright, 2017). While a quantitative nonexperimental approach may yield limited results because the researcher does not gather pre- and post-test data, a nonexperimental approach is most widely used by doctoral quantitative researchers (Bhattacherjee, 2012),

> This researcher drew on the three theories: the LMX (Dansereau et al., 1975); the TMX

(Seers, 1989); and the knowledge sharing theory (Nonaka, 1994). Hoefer and Green (2016) noted that the constructs of existing theories could be used to develop new research models. Based on the recommendations of Hoefer and Green, the researcher developed a model to explore the influence of the vertical interactions between IT governance personnel and software development team members (i.e., negotiation), and the horizontal interactions between team members (i.e., reciprocity) on knowledge-sharing in software development teams. By using the research chosen research design, the researcher could quantify the impact of the independent variables of negotiation and reciprocity on the dependent variable of knowledge sharing (see

Field, 2013; Sekaran & Bougie, 2014; Vogt, 2007).

The researcher hired Qualtrics, an online survey company, to recruit 85 qualified participants to participate in the study. The researcher had no direct contact with any of the participants. Participants responded to a total of 35 questions on the survey where variables were measured using a Likert-type scale. The use of Likert-type scales to operationalize variables is common in the scholarly literature (see Bala et al., 2017; Chatterjee, Moody, Lowry, Chakraborty, & Hardin, 2015; Valacich, Wang, & Jessup, 2018). The 35 survey questions included seven items from the LMX instrument that measured the negotiation construct. A total of 10 questions measured the variable reciprocity-exchange of ideas, four questions measured reciprocity-meetings, and four questions measured reciprocity-cohesiveness. Additionally, 10 questions measured the knowledge-sharing variable. The researcher then used a multiple regression analysis to analyze the collected data and test the study's hypobook (see Gregor &

Klein, 2014; Iyer, 2017).

Target Population and Sample

Field (2013) referred to a target population as a collection of all objects of interest to researchers. In the present study, the target population consisted of software developers who worked in the United States, had a college degree and possessed at least two years of software development experience. Field noted that researchers use inferences drawn from the results of data analyses to describe the characteristics of a target population.

Target populations can be quite large. Hadullo, Oboko, and Omwenga (2018) identified their target population as the entire e-learning population in Kenya. When identifying a target population, it is important to ensure that the sample frame is representative of the population of interest. Kilic (2018) conducted a study for the nursing students attending classes in two universities in Turkey. A total of 235 students, representing a response rate of 96.59%, participated in Kilic's study. However, Kilic failed to report the sample frame and the population of the study, reducing the generalizability of the study's findings. The following sections provide specifics on the study's population, sample, and power analysis.

Population

McClave, Benson, and Sincich (2014) defined population as an established group of interest to a researcher. With social science and management research, people are the target subject of interest (McClave et al., 2014). According to Capella University, people are the preferred terms to refer to the entire population of all participants. Compeau, Marcolin, Kelley, and Higgins (2012) cited the necessity for providing a specific description of the target population to allow for the generalization of the data analysis results. The present researcher's goal was to extrapolate insights from survey data using multiple regression analyses to determine whether negotiation and reciprocity influenced the knowledge-sharing processes of United States software developers. Therefore, identifying the population as all software developers in the United States would help readers to know the scope of the generalization of the study's results (Compeau et al., 2012).

According to US-Software-Developers (2012), there were around 1,020,000 software developers in 2012 in the United States. From the population of 1,020,000 software developers, the researcher calculated simple random sampling using G*Power. This calculation is discussed in detail in a later section of this chapter. Because the scope of this study was the entire United States software developer population, it was necessary for the population, the sample frame, and the sample of 85 software developers to share the same characteristics (Compeau et al., 2012). Goode and Cruise (2006) and Madarie (2017) noted the importance of ensuring alignment between the sample frame and the target population. The following section contains information on the sample and the sample frame.

Sample

Vogt (2007) noted that verification of the sample frame was necessary to ensure the selected sample came from the best possible group of people to represent the target population. Thus, researchers must ensure that the characteristics of the sample frame are the same as the characteristics of the target population (George et al., 2017). This researcher hired Qualtrics, an online survey company to provide the study's sample frame. Qualtrics has a database of participants from across the United States, and this allowed the researcher to ensure that the sample frame for this study was representative of the target population.

This researcher provided Qualtrics with the study's selection criteria to determine if the company could provide an adequate sample frame from their member database. Qualtrics indicated that their member database contained a total of 17,640 verified software developers that met the study's selection criteria. Sekaran and Bougie (2014) asserted that when the chosen sample frame is large and has the same characteristics of the target population, that the sample frame is suitable for selecting research participants. From the sample frame of 17,640 software developers in their member database, Qualtrics randomly selected individuals to receive invitations to participate in the study. The selection criteria ensured that each participant was a United States citizens, worked on a software development team as a programmer, had a minimum of a two-year college degree, and had a minimum of two years of experience working as a programmer. The random sampling process continued until Qualtrics had collected the minimum required number of complete survey responses. The following section presents the details of the power analysis used to calculate sample size.

Power Analysis

Researchers calculate the power of the sample to determine whether the data analysis results collected from a sample are representative of the population (Vogt, 2007).

Thus, through careful sampling, a researcher could reduce the gap between the research sample and the target population. Field (2013) argued that a smaller, carefully selected sample could effectively be used to generalize findings to a target population. Sekaran and Bougie (2014) also supported this assertion.

Faul, Erdfelder, Buchner, and Lang (2009) said that G*Power version 3.1.9 could be used to determine the estimated sample size to detect significant statistical results using multiple linear regression analyses. The researcher used parameters identified by Cohen (1992) to calculate the minimum sample size necessary to ensure the study's findings were valid. Cohen noted that with the conventional $a = .05$ and a power of .80, a researcher could produce significant statistical results from the responses of 85 participants. Thus, the researcher ensured that Qualtrics collected survey responses from a minimum of 85 randomly selected participants.

Procedures

What follows is a description of the procedures that this researcher adopted for this study.

The following sections cover procedures used to select participants and collect and analyze data.

First, the procedures used to select the participants are discussed.

Participant Selection

Qualtrics randomly selected participants from its participant database using inclusion criteria the researcher provided to the survey company. Qualtrics e-mailed database members who met the selection criteria providing them with a link to a Web page that explained the purpose of the study and invited them to participate. Each participant needed to (a) be United States citizens, (b) be working on a software development team as a programmer, (c) have a minimum of a two-year college degree, and (d) have a minimum of two years of experience in their role as a programmer. On the survey Web page, Qualtrics provided prospective participants with the study's informed consent information. When participants indicated they accepted the informed consent information, they were able to enter the survey. If database members did not indicate they understood and accepted the informed consent information, the system displayed a thank you note, and the system prevented them from entering the survey. The Qualtrics Company recruited a total of 85 participants.

Protection of Participants

The researcher took several steps to protect participants. The researcher protected participants by using a third-party survey company. Participants can experience fear or agitation when asked to respond honestly to survey questions. The fact participants were members of Qualtrics' database diminished the potential for these feelings. As part of that membership, database members had volunteered to participate in survey research and been verified as members. Furthermore, all participation was voluntary, the survey process guaranteed participants anonymity, none of the participants provided personal information.

As Qualtrics recruited participants directly from their participant database, the researcher had no personal contact with those invited to take part in the study. This process maintained participant anonymity and added an extra level of protection when selecting participants. Participant recruitment via a third party also offers an extra level of assurance to participants that it is safe to mark their responses honestly and accurately (Hunter et al., 2018; Wallace &

Sheldon, 2015). After the completion of the survey process, the researcher received a file from Qualtrics that contained only the survey responses, and this file did not include any identifying information that could be linked to individual database members.

Data Collection

Before displaying the final survey to the participants, the researcher downloaded, reviewed, and proofread the entire survey as it would be presented to the participants. Following the recruitment of qualified participants, Qualtrics sent the participants a URL link to the survey that was published on Qualtrics' website. Upon visiting the survey page, participants were asked to accept the informed consent form. Once they had done so, each participant answered the 35 survey questions. If a response was not indicated, the system displayed a text message and deactivated the *submit* button, preventing the participants who did not answer all the questions from continuing with the survey. If a participant did not fully complete the survey before logging off, the result was an incomplete survey. The resulting data did not include any incomplete surveys. Data collection continued until there were 85 completed surveys.

Once the minimum number of surveys had been obtained, Qualtrics informed the researcher via email that the data collection was complete. Qualtrics sent the researcher a link to download the collected data. The researcher logged into the Qualtrics website and downloaded an IBM SPSS version 24 file containing the data from the 85 completed surveys. As per Capella University requirements, the researcher will safely store the data on a standalone computer that has no access to the Internet for seven years, after which time the researcher will delete all data.

Data Analysis

The researcher used IBM SPSS version 24 software to evaluate the data. Subsequently, the researcher conducted hypothesis testing for each research subquestion. Before beginning data analysis, the researcher examined the data to remove outliers. According to Sekaran and Bougie (2014) and Vogt (2007), descriptive statistics help researchers explore their quantitative data in a manageable way by using means and standard deviations. The purpose of a descriptive statistic is to examine the quality of the data and find problems (Sekaran & Bougie, 2014; Vogt, 2007). After running the descriptive statistics, the researcher then ran multiple linear regression analyses for each of the five variables to determine

a *p*-value (Vogt, 2007). Researchers can use correlations to

illustrate a relationship among variables. With inferential

statistics, a researcher could use existing data for making a

prediction based on the knowledge gained from the analyses

of the collected raw data (Vogt, 2007). Researchers can use the

graphics derived from descriptive statistics to determine if

there is a linear relationship between two variables (Vogt,

2007).

Instruments

The researcher used three previously published

instruments to collect data about negotiation, reciprocity, and

knowledge sharing. This researcher incorporated three

instruments: the 7-item LMX instrument (Sollitto et al., 2016),

the TMX instrument (de Jong et al., 2014) and Nonaka's

knowledge-sharing instrument (Choi, 2016; Nonaka, 1994) to

measure five variables: negotiation, reciprocity-exchange of

ideas, reciprocity-meetings, reciprocity-cohesiveness, and

knowledge sharing. The following sections address the history of each instrument separately.

The 7-Item LMX Instrument

For measuring negotiation, the researcher used the 7-item LMX instrument. The LMX instrument was based on the LMX theory introduced by Dansereau et al. (1975). Dansereau et al. used the LMX theory to describe the relationships between supervisors and subordinates. The concept is based on in-group and out-group status (Dansereau et al., 1975). The dyadic relationships between a supervisor and an employee can be used to determine whether an employee is assigned to an in-group or an out-group. The researcher used the seven-item LMX instrument for negotiation, which was similar to what Sollitto et al. (2016) used. This research produced statistically comparable results with the results of Sollitto et al. The instrument was a conversion of each construct into a list of questions to which participants responded. Thus, an operational definition was the reduction of an abstract construct into a list of questions to collect data via the survey.

The LMX instrument was in the public domain, so the researcher was not required to obtain permission from the authors before using it in the present study.

TMX Instrument

The researcher used 18 questions from the TMX instrument to measure reciprocity. Ten of those questions measured the variable reciprocity-exchange of ideas, four questions measured the variable reciprocity-meetings, and four questions measured the variable reciprocitycohesiveness. The TMX instrument converted each construct into a list of questions to which participants responded. This process allows researchers to operationalize the constructs and collect data via a survey. The present researcher's use of the TMX instrument aligned with previous research by de Jong et al. (2014). This researcher produced statistically comparable results with the results of de Jong et al. when using the TMX instrument. The TMX instrument was in the public domain, so the researcher was not required to obtain permission from the authors before using it in the present study.

Nonaka's Knowledge-Sharing Instrument

Nonaka (1994) developed a knowledge-sharing instrument based on Anderson's (1983) adaptive control of thought model for knowledge conversion. According to Nonaka (1994), there are four modes of knowledge conversion: (a) from tacit knowledge to tacit knowledge (socialization), (b) from explicit knowledge to explicit knowledge (combination), (c) from tacit knowledge to explicit knowledge (externalization), and (d) from explicit knowledge to tacit knowledge (internalization). This researcher used 10 questions from the knowledge-sharing instrument developed by Nonaka. Choi (2016) also used Nonaka's knowledge sharing instrument, indicating it was a validated instrument. The Knowledge sharing instrument was in the public domain, so the researcher was not required to obtain permission from the author before using it in the present study. The following sections contain information on the validity and reliability of the instruments used to collect the data.

Validity

Validity is a concern when selecting an instrument to collect data from participants (Vogt, 2007). Validity deals with the suitability of an instrument for the targeted participants to collect data aligned with the objectives of the research (Field, 2013). This researcher studied constructs from the LMX, the TMX, and the knowledge-sharing theory. Researchers such as Sollitto et al. (2016), de Jong et al. (2014), and Choi (2016) also studied the same constructs using the same instruments. Replicability is the most powerful single evidence of validity (Vogt, 2007), and the use of the instruments in different studies demonstrate that the instruments are legitimate in terms of their validity and reliability.

To test validity, Cacioppo and Petty (1982) demonstrated that a correlation existed between the scores of their subjects and the scores of standardized academic tests.

Therefore the results of their test were validated. This researcher used a matrix scatterplot to validate the data. Figure 2 presents the matrix scatterplot. As depicted in Figure 2, the researcher plotted the regression standardized predicted value against the regression standardized residual value. Researchers use matrix scatterplot charts to test validity (Field, 2013). Ideally, when these conditions are met, the scatterplot depicts no specific patterns. Conversely, a scatterplot can show the violation of assumptions if there are clusters near either side of the graph or if there is a nonlinear pattern. The researcher observed no such extreme concentrations.

For this study, the validity of the most suitable instrument is the one that is closely related to the vertical relationship between a supervisor and their subordinates (Riddell & Song, 2017). For the horizontal relationships among team members, the validity of the most suitable instrument is the one that is closely related to the relationships among team members (Riddell & Song, 2017). The researcher executed multiple linear regression analyses using IBM SPSS version 24, and the results showed correlation patterns among the variables. These patterns are an indication of the validity of the selected instruments (Riddell & Song, 2017).

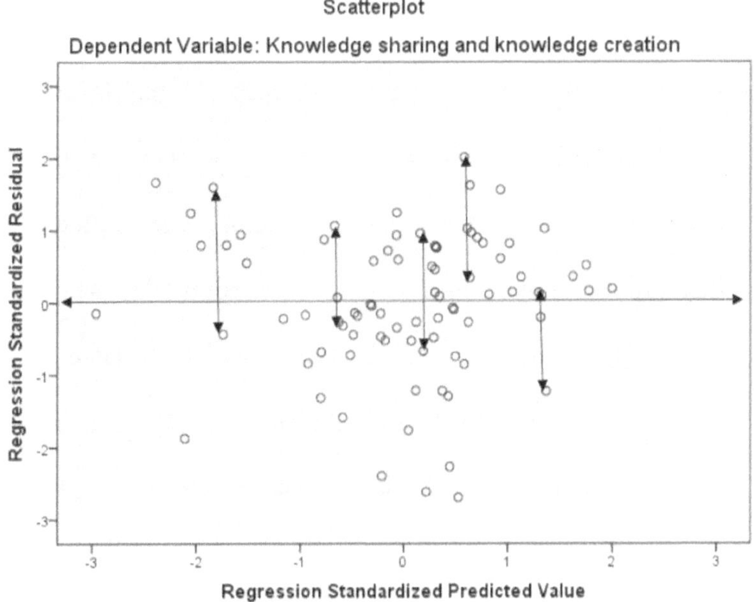

Figure 2. Matrix scatterplot.

Reliability

The internal reliability of an instrument is an indication of the absence of errors (Sekaran & Bougie, 2014). If the absence of errors is consistent with the instrument's measurements across different social settings and time, researchers can deem an instrument to be reliable as reliability refers to the stability and consistency of the instrument (Sekaran & Bougie, 2014). This researcher noticed that the collected data from the three instruments, when reflected in histograms, showed clusters of the data properties (see Field, 2013). Data clustering is a measurement of a related set of items within an instrument (Sekaran & Bougie, 2014). Reliability is the interpretation of the collected data using the chosen instrument.

> Replicability in a different social setting is evidence of reliability (Vogt, 2007).

Researchers also use Cronbach's alpha to find correlations between several measured items and to validate the internal consistency of questionnaires (Bhattacherjee, 2012; Saide, Rahmat, Hsiao-Lan, Okfalisa, & Wirdah, 2017; Sekaran & Bougie, 2014; Vogt, 2007). This researcher used IBM SPSS Statistics version 24 to generate Cronbach's alpha scores to measure the instrument's reliability. The level of reliability for the variables was .70 or higher, except for the variable of reciprocity-cohesiveness. The purpose of providing detailed information about the research design was to empower future researchers to locate their instruments with less effort and replicate the study if necessary.

Ethical Considerations

The researcher adhered to the rules of Capella University's Institutional Review Board when taking measures to protect the study's participants. The researcher hired Qualtrics, an independent research company, to recruit and select 85 participants to respond to the survey. The researcher had no direct contact with those invited to take part in the study. This measure safeguarded participants' anonymity. The file the researcher received from Qualtrics contained only the participant responses, and it did not include any identifying informa

tion that would compromise the participants' anonymity. Although the risk to participants was small, answering some questions about team interfaces might cause a respondent to recall an event in the past that could trigger uneasiness (Ritchie, Skowronski, Cadogan, & Sedikides, 2014). Additionally, the participation in this research was entirely voluntary. The researcher exercised extreme caution to cause no harm, to act with beneficence, and protect the collected data. The protection of human subjects in research is a primary fundamental goal of schools and government agencies.

The Secretary of the United States Department of Health and Human Services commissioned and published *The Belmont Report* (1979) to address the need for the protection of human subjects in research. The report declared the need for balancing scientific research with the social benefit and the mandatory requirements for protecting human participants. Even when acting ethically, conflicts could arise that compromise the ethical behaviors of the researcher or pose risks to the participants (Creswell, 2014). Thus it is vital to remember that researchers are entirely responsible for their practices, actions, and communications with the participants. Researchers must protect a study's participants from harm and guard the confidentiality of any personally identifying information. Additionally, researchers should avoid exerting direct or indirect pressure on participants when making an effort to persuade them to enroll in a study.

The fundamental objective of *The Belmont Report* (1979) was the protection of participants from harm. The report promoted the assessment of risks and benefits to research subjects. Capella University's IRB has the authority to review, modify, approve, or reject a student's research proposal based on concerns about the protection of the human subjects and imbalances in risk-benefit criteria. It is necessary for any study that includes human participants to be reviewed by an IRB to ensure that the research adheres to *The Belmont Report's* principles. The fundamental principles for protecting human subjects include respect for persons, beneficence, and justice. These principles balance the burden of the research against any gained benefits.

The present researcher was required to provide an informed consent form and secure each participant's acceptance of that document before collecting any data. Creswell noted that a subtle risk could rise from the misalignment of the understanding of the purpose of the investigation between a researcher and one or more of the participants. Creswell (2014) referred to this misunderstanding as a deception. A solution for mitigating the risk of deception is the adherence to the rule of IRB to assess the readability of the informed consent document. The informed consent form should be written at the 8th-grade reading level to ensure it is comprehensible to all potential respondents.

This researcher relied heavily on IRB documentation, Capella University's dissertation guide, and external resources such as guidelines from the Academy of Management (AOM, 2015). The researcher attempted to understand the magnitude, the depth, and the extent of the expected ethical behaviors and actions. There was no predetermined ethical manual. Researchers should avoid deviation from ethical regulations (AOM, 2015). However, the AOM did not identify the boundary of the variation. Furthermore, according to the AOM, the ethical considerations when conducting research do not include potential risks. Jeanes (2017) asserted that the limit of protecting participants falls entirely on the shoulders of the researchers.

Jeanes (2017) addressed the balancing of explicit ethical requirements and the inherent nature of ethics. The author advocated that researchers must be concerned with ethics when selecting procedural processes. Jeanes reviewed scholarly articles on research ethics and the role of management. Jeanes reviewed the literature concerning management dilemmas and the challenging elements of negotiation. Jeanes identified different ethical challenges facing researchers and managers.

Jeanes (2017) argued that researchers deal with ethics regarding privacy by protecting their participants and avoiding deception. Jeanes (2017) noted that ethical subjectivity is sometimes difficult due to the formal process of research. Jeanes recruited established researchers for interviews and found that not all participants blamed IRB for impairing the review process. Jeanes assessed that despite the challenges faced when seeking approval from the IRB, most researchers did not neglect their responsibility toward their participants in the research.

Summary

Chapter 3 included information on the study's purpose, research questions, research design, procedures, instruments, and ethical considerations. By carefully outlining the methodology used to conduct the study, future researchers can replicate the study if necessary.

Chapter 4 includes the results of data collection and analysis.

9 783384 438799